MAX LUCADO

LIFE LESSONS *from*

JOHN

When God Became Man

PREPARED BY THE LIVINGSTONE CORPORATION

Harper*Christian*
Resources

Life Lessons from John
© 2018 by Max Lucado

Requests for information should be addressed to:
HarperChristian Resources, 3900 Sparks Dr. SE, Grand Rapids, Michigan 49546

ISBN 978-0-310-08636-9 (softcover)
ISBN 978-0-310-08637-6 (ebook)

Produced with the assistance of the Livingstone Corporation (www.livingstonecorp.com). Project staff includes Jake Barton, Joel Bartlett, Andy Culbertson, Mary Horner Collins, and Will Reaves.

Editor: Neil Wilson

First Printing December 2017 / Printed in the United States of America

CONTENTS

HOW TO STUDY THE BIBLE

The Bible is a peculiar book. Words crafted in another language. Deeds done in a distant era. Events recorded in a far-off land. Counsel offered to a foreign people. It is a peculiar book.

It's surprising that anyone reads it. It's too old. Some of its writings date back 5,000 years. It's too bizarre. The book speaks of incredible floods, fires, earthquakes, and people with supernatural abilities. It's too radical. The Bible calls for undying devotion to a carpenter who called himself God's Son.

Logic says this book shouldn't survive. Too old, too bizarre, too radical.

The Bible has been banned, burned, scoffed, and ridiculed. Scholars have mocked it as foolish. Kings have branded it as illegal. A thousand times over the grave has been dug and the dirge has begun, but somehow the Bible never stays in the grave. Not only has it survived, but it has also thrived. It is the single most popular book in all of history. It has been the bestselling book in the world for years!

There is no way on earth to explain it. Which perhaps is the only explanation. For the Bible's durability is not found on *earth* but in *heaven*. The millions who have tested its claims and claimed its promises know there is but one answer: the Bible is God's book and God's voice.

As you read it, you would be wise to give some thought to two questions: *What is the purpose of the Bible?* and *How do I study the Bible?* Time spent reflecting on these two issues will greatly enhance your Bible study.

What is the purpose of the Bible?

Let the Bible itself answer that question: "*From infancy you have known the Holy Scriptures, which are able to make you wise for salvation through faith in Christ Jesus*" (2 Timothy 3:15).

The purpose of the Bible? Salvation. God's highest passion is to get his children home. His book, the Bible, describes his plan of salvation. The purpose of the Bible is to proclaim God's plan and passion to save his children.

This is the reason why this book has endured through the centuries. It dares to tackle the toughest questions about life: *Where do I go after I die? Is there a God? What do I do with my fears?* The Bible is the treasure map that leads to God's highest treasure—eternal life.

But how do you study the Bible? Countless copies of Scripture sit unread on bookshelves and nightstands simply because people don't know how to read it. What can you do to make the Bible real in your life?

The clearest answer is found in the words of Jesus: "*Ask and it will be given to you; seek and you will find; knock and the door will be opened to you*" (Matthew 7:7).

The first step in understanding the Bible is asking God to help you. You should read it prayerfully. If anyone understands God's Word, it is because of God and not the reader.

"*The Advocate, the Holy Spirit, whom the Father will send in my name, will teach you all things and will remind you of everything I have said to you*" (John 14:26).

Before reading the Bible, pray and invite God to speak to you. Don't go to Scripture looking for your idea, but go searching for his.

Not only should you read the Bible prayerfully, but you should also read it carefully. "*Seek and you will find*" is the pledge. The Bible is not a newspaper to be skimmed but rather a mine to be quarried. "*If you look for it as for silver and search for it as for hidden treasure, then you will understand the fear of the* LORD *and find the knowledge of God"* (Proverbs 2:4–5).

Any worthy find requires effort. The Bible is no exception. To understand the Bible, you don't have to be brilliant, but you must be willing to roll up your sleeves and search.

"Do your best to present yourself to God as one approved, a worker who does not need to be ashamed and who correctly handles the word of truth" (2 Timothy 2:15).

Here's a practical point. Study the Bible a bit at a time. Hunger is not satisfied by eating twenty-one meals in one sitting once a week. The body needs a steady diet to remain strong. So does the soul. When God sent food to his people in the wilderness, he didn't provide loaves already made. Instead, he sent them manna in the shape of *"thin flakes like frost on the ground"* (Exodus 16:14).

God gave manna in limited portions.

God sends spiritual food the same way. He opens the heavens with just enough nutrients for today's hunger. He provides *"a rule for this, a rule for that; a little here, a little there"* (Isaiah 28:10).

Don't be discouraged if your reading reaps a small harvest. Some days a lesser portion is all that is needed. What is important is to search every day for that day's message. A steady diet of God's Word over a lifetime builds a healthy soul and mind.

It's much like the little girl who returned from her first day at school feeling a bit dejected. Her mom asked, "Did you learn anything?"

"Apparently not enough," the girl responded. "I have to go back tomorrow, and the next day, and the next . . . "

Such is the case with learning. And such is the case with Bible study. Understanding comes little by little over a lifetime.

There is a third step in understanding the Bible. After the asking and seeking comes the knocking. After you ask and search, *"knock and the door will be opened to you"* (Matthew 7:7).

To knock is to stand at God's door. To make yourself available. To climb the steps, cross the porch, stand at the doorway, and volunteer.

Knocking goes beyond the realm of thinking and into the realm of acting.

To knock is to ask, *What can I do? How can I obey? Where can I go?*

It's one thing to know what to do. It's another to do it. But for those who do it—those who choose to obey—a special reward awaits them.

"Whoever looks intently into the perfect law that gives freedom, and continues in it—not forgetting what they have heard, but doing it—they will be blessed in what they do" (James 1:25).

What a promise. Blessings come to those who do what they read in God's Word! It's the same with medicine. If you only read the label but ignore the pills, it won't help. It's the same with food. If you only read the recipe but never cook, you won't be fed. And it's the same with the Bible. If you only read the words but never obey, you'll never know the joy God has promised.

Ask. Search. Knock. Simple, isn't it? So why don't you give it a try? If you do, you'll see why the Bible is the most remarkable book in history.

INTRODUCTION TO
The Gospel of John

H e's an old man, this one who sits on the stool and leans against the wall. Eyes closed and face soft. Were it not for his hand stroking his beard, you'd think he was asleep.

Some in the room assume he is. He does this often during worship. As the people sing, his eyes will close and his chin will fall until it rests on his chest, and there he will remain motionless. Silent.

Those who know him well know better. They know he is not resting. He is traveling. Atop the music he journeys back, back, back until he is young again. Strong again. There again. There on the seashore with James and the apostles. There on the trail with the disciples and the women. There in the temple with Caiaphas and the accusers.

It's been sixty years, but John sees him still. The decades took John's strength, but they didn't take his memory. The years dulled his sight, but they didn't dull his vision. The seasons may have wrinkled his face, but they didn't soften his love.

He had been with God. God had been with him. How could he forget? The wine that moments before had been water—John could still taste it.

The mud placed on the eyes of the blind man in Jerusalem—John could still remember it.

The aroma of Mary's perfume as it filled the room—John could still smell it. And the voice. Oh, the voice. His voice. John could still hear it.

I am the light of the world . . . I am the door . . . I am the way, the truth, the life.

I will come back and take you to be with me.

Those who believe in me will have life even if they die.

John could hear him. John could see him. Scenes branded on his heart. Words seared into his soul. John would never forget. How could he? He had been there.

He opens his eyes and blinks. The singing has stopped. The teaching has begun. John looks at the listeners and listens to the teacher.

If only you could have been there, he thinks.

But most of the people here weren't even born then. And most who were with Jesus are dead. Peter is gone. So is James. Nathaniel, Martha, Bartholomew. They are all gone. Even Paul, the apostle who came late, is dead.

Only John remains.

He looks again at the church. Small but earnest. They lean forward to hear the teacher. John listens to him. What a task. Speaking of one he never saw. Explaining words he never heard. John is there if the teacher needs him.

But what will happen when John is gone? What will the teacher do then? When John's voice is silent and his tongue stilled? Who will tell them how Jesus silenced the waves? Will they hear how he fed the thousands? Will they remember how he prayed for unity?

How will they know? If only they could have been there. Suddenly, in his heart he knows what to do.

Later, under the light of a sunlit shaft, the old fisherman unfolds the scroll and begins to write the story of his life . . .

In the beginning was the Word . . .

AUTHOR AND DATE

John, who along with Peter and James, was a member of Jesus' "inner circle" of disciples. As such, he was given access to events such as the raising of Jairus' daughter (see Luke 8:49–51), Jesus' Transfiguration (see Matthew 17:1–2), and Jesus' agony in the Garden of Gethsemane (see Mark 14:32–34). John, along with his father, Zebedee, and his brother James, were fishermen when Jesus called them (see Matthew 4:18). Jesus referred to the two brothers as "sons of thunder," perhaps due to their tendency at times to speak out like an untamed storm (see Luke 9:51–56). John, for his part, often referred to himself as "the disciple whom Jesus loved" (see John 13:23; 19:26; 21:7). It is believed John wrote his Gospel c. AD 65–95.

SITUATION

Irenaeus, an early church father writing in the second century, wrote that John "published the Gospel while he was resident at Ephesus in Asia." The fact that John does not include major events listed in Matthew, Mark, and Luke (the "Synoptics"), while including episodes not mentioned in those Gospels, have led scholars to conclude that John wrote his Gospel as a more reflective presentation of major themes in Jesus' life and ministry. It is clear that John's purpose in writing was to relate his testimony of Christ, so that his readers "may believe that Jesus is the Messiah, the Son of God, and . . . may have life in his name" (John 20:31).

KEY THEMES

- Jesus was and is eternally present in spirit.
- While Jesus was on earth, he communicated with many kinds of people about his mission.
- Jesus performed many miracles to show the nature of his love and power.
- Jesus prepared his followers for the future by promising them the presence of the Holy Spirit.

KEY VERSES

In the beginning was the Word, and the Word was with God, and the Word was God (John 1:1).

CONTENTS

WHEN GOD BECAME MAN

The Word became flesh and made his dwelling among us. We have seen his glory, the glory of the one and only Son, who came from the Father, full of grace and truth.

JOHN 1:14

REFLECTION

Christ was born on earth by the will of God, and when we accept him as our Savior, we are also "born again" through the will of God. This our second birth—our spiritual birth into eternal life. What are some of the events surrounding your second birth in Christ?

_____

_____

_____

_____

SITUATION

The language and tone of John's writing is quite different from the Gospels of Matthew, Mark and Luke, but the subject is the same: *Jesus Christ*. The first three words of John's Gospel echo the very first verse of the Bible: "In the beginning . . ." (Genesis 1:1). The Gospels of Matthew and Luke highlight Jesus' human lineage, while John highlights his divine nature. From the start, John sets Jesus in the center of God's eternal plan for the world.

OBSERVATION

*Read John 1:1–18 from the New International
Version or the New King James Version.*

New International Version
¹ In the beginning was the Word, and the Word was with God, and the Word was God. ² He was with God in the beginning. ³ Through him all things were made; without him nothing was made that has been made. ⁴ In him was life, and that life was the light of all mankind. ⁵ The light shines in the darkness, and the darkness has not overcome it.

⁶ There was a man sent from God whose name was John. ⁷ He came as a witness to testify concerning that light, so that through him all might believe. ⁸ He himself was not the light; he came only as a witness to the light.

⁹ The true light that gives light to everyone was coming into the world. ¹⁰ He was in the world, and though the world was made through him, the world did not recognize him. ¹¹ He came to that which was his own, but his own did not receive him. ¹² Yet to all who did receive him, to those who believed in his name, he gave the right to become children of God— ¹³ children born not of natural descent, nor of human decision or a husband's will, but born of God.

¹⁴ The Word became flesh and made his dwelling among us. We have seen his glory, the glory of the one and only Son, who came from the Father, full of grace and truth.

¹⁵ (John testified concerning him. He cried out, saying, "This is the one I spoke about when I said, 'He who comes after me has surpassed me because he was before me.'")¹⁶ Out of his fullness we have all received grace in place of grace already given. ¹⁷ For the law was given through Moses; grace and truth came through Jesus Christ. ¹⁸ No one has ever seen God, but the one and only Son, who is himself God and is in closest relationship with the Father, has made him known.

New King James Version

¹ In the beginning was the Word, and the Word was with God, and the Word was God. ² He was in the beginning with God. ³ All things were made through Him, and without Him nothing was made that was made. ⁴ In Him was life, and the life was the light of men. ⁵ And the light shines in the darkness, and the darkness did not comprehend it.

⁶ There was a man sent from God, whose name was John. ⁷ This man came for a witness, to bear witness of the Light, that all through him might believe. ⁸ He was not that Light, but was sent to bear witness of that Light. ⁹ That was the true Light which gives light to every man coming into the world.

[10] He was in the world, and the world was made through Him, and the world did not know Him. [11] He came to His own, and His own did not receive Him. [12] But as many as received Him, to them He gave the right to become children of God, to those who believe in His name: [13] who were born, not of blood, nor of the will of the flesh, nor of the will of man, but of God.

[14] And the Word became flesh and dwelt among us, and we beheld His glory, the glory as of the only begotten of the Father, full of grace and truth.

[15] John bore witness of Him and cried out, saying, "This was He of whom I said, 'He who comes after me is preferred before me, for He was before me.'"

[16] And of His fullness we have all received, and grace for grace. [17] For the law was given through Moses, but grace and truth came through Jesus Christ. [18] No one has seen God at any time. The only begotten Son, who is in the bosom of the Father, He has declared Him.

EXPLORATION

1. Why do you think John begins his Gospel by stating that Jesus was with God in the very beginning—at the time of creation? What is he communicating to his readers?

_____

_____

_____

2. What does this passage reveal about Jesus' mission?

_____

_____

_____

3. What was John the Baptist's purpose as it relates to Jesus coming into this world?

_____

_____

_____

4. Many people did not recognize Jesus as the Messiah or believe that he was God's Son. What did they miss by not receiving him?

_____

_____

_____

5. John tells us that Jesus "came from the Father, full of grace and truth" (verse 14). How has this grace and truth benefitted your life?

_____

_____

_____

6. What does Jesus' life as a man tell us about God as Father?

_____

_____

_____

INSPIRATION

It all happened in a moment, a most remarkable moment.

As moments go, that one appeared no different than any other. If you could somehow pick it up off the timeline and examine it, it would look exactly like the ones that have passed while you have read these words. It came and it went. It was preceded and succeeded by others just like it. It was one of the countless moments that have marked time since eternity became measurable.

But in reality, that particular moment was like none other. For through that segment of time a spectacular thing occurred. God became a man. While the creatures of earth walked unaware, Divinity arrived. Heaven opened herself and placed her most precious one in a human womb.

The omnipotent, in one instant, made himself breakable. He who had been spirit became pierceable. He who was larger than the universe became an embryo. And he who sustains the world with a word chose to be dependent upon the nourishment of a young girl.

God as a fetus. Holiness sleeping in a womb. The creator of life being created.

God was given eyebrows, elbows, two kidneys, and a spleen. He stretched against the walls and floated in the amniotic fluids of his mother.

God had come near.

He came, not as a flash of light or as an unapproachable conqueror, but as one whose first cries were heard by a peasant girl and a sleepy carpenter. The hands that first held him were unmanicured, calloused, and dirty.

No silk. No ivory. No hype. No party. No hoopla.

Were it not for the shepherds, there would have been no reception. And were it not for a group of stargazers, there would have been no gifts.

Angels watched as Mary changed God's diaper. The universe watched with wonder as The Almighty learned to walk. Children played in the street with him. And had the synagogue leader in Nazareth known who was listening to his sermons . . .

For thirty-three years he would feel everything you and I have ever felt. He felt weak. He grew weary. He was afraid of failure. He was susceptible to wooing women. He got colds, burped, and had body odor. His feelings got hurt. His feet got tired. And his head ached.

To think of Jesus in such a light is—well, it seems almost irreverent, doesn't it? It's not something we like to do; it's uncomfortable. It is much easier to keep the humanity out of the incarnation. Clean the manure from around the manger.

Wipe the sweat out of his eyes. Pretend he never snored or blew his nose or hit his thumb with a hammer.

He's easier to stomach that way. There is something about keeping him divine that keeps him distant, packaged, predictable.

But don't do it. For heaven's sake, don't. Let him be as human as he intended to be. Let him into the mire and muck of our world. For only if we let him in can he pull us out. (From *God Came Near* by Max Lucado.)

REACTION

7. What surprises you about Jesus coming to earth as a human being?

_____

_____

_____

8. What is comforting or encouraging about God taking on a human form?

_____

_____

_____

9. In what way does this truth inspire you?

_____

_____

_____

10. What does Jesus' willingness to become a human being reveal about his heart?

_____

_____

_____

11. In what ways would your life be different if Jesus had not yet come to earth?

_____

_____

_____

12. How will you be a witness to others of the light that Jesus brought into this world?

_____

_____

_____

LIFE LESSONS

John introduces his Gospel as the ultimate life lesson. One of Jesus' attributes that he highlights is the fact that Jesus is *life*. He offers true life. He offers eternal life. As you will discover throughout these lessons, the prologue of John acts like an overture in a symphony. The themes you've just begun to think about will be examined repeatedly in the lessons to come. This study is an opportunity to know Life as you've never known him before.

DEVOTION

Lord God, we come to you, thankful that you have pierced our world. You became flesh and dwelled among us. You saw us in our fallen state, and you reached in and pulled us out. You offered us salvation and mercy. We thank you for what you have done for us.

JOURNALING

How does the light of God shine in your life every day?

_____

_____

_____

_____

_____

_____

FOR FURTHER READING

To complete the book of John during this twelve-part study, read John 1:1–34. For more Bible passages about God becoming a man, read 1 Corinthians 8:5–6; Galatians 4:4; Philippians 2:7–8; 1 Timothy 3:16; Hebrews 2:14; and 1 John 1:1–2.

A WEDDING IN CANA

His mother said to the servants,
"Whatever He says to you, do it."
JOHN 2:5 NKJV

REFLECTION

The fact that Jesus showed up for a wedding in Cana, where he performed his first miracle, makes it a deeply significant event. Think of the most memorable wedding you have attended. What in particular made it stand out to you?

_____

_____

_____

_____

_____

SITUATION

Weddings in Jesus' day were extended community events that often lasted a week or more. Hospitality ruled the day, and families were under significant social pressure to provide lavishly for their guests. So, when the wine ran out at the wedding feast Jesus was attending, it created a major crisis for the family of the bride and groom. Mary tried to help by enlisting her son's assistance in finding a solution. Even she probably didn't expect the results that followed.

OBSERVATION

Read John 2:1–11 from the New International
Version or the New King James Version.

NEW INTERNATIONAL VERSION
¹ On the third day a wedding took place at Cana in Galilee. Jesus' mother was there,² and Jesus and his disciples had also been invited to the wedding. ³ When the wine was gone, Jesus' mother said to him, "They have no more wine."

⁴ "Woman, why do you involve me?" Jesus replied. "My hour has not yet come."

⁵ His mother said to the servants, "Do whatever he tells you."

⁶ Nearby stood six stone water jars, the kind used by the Jews for ceremonial washing, each holding from twenty to thirty gallons.

⁷ Jesus said to the servants, "Fill the jars with water"; so they filled them to the brim.

⁸ Then he told them, "Now draw some out and take it to the master of the banquet."

They did so, ⁹ and the master of the banquet tasted the water that had been turned into wine. He did not realize where it had come from, though the servants who had drawn the water knew. Then he called the bridegroom aside ¹⁰ and said, "Everyone brings out the choice wine first and then the cheaper wine after the guests have had too much to drink; but you have saved the best till now."

¹¹ What Jesus did here in Cana of Galilee was the first of the signs through which he revealed his glory; and his disciples believed in him.

New King James Version

¹ On the third day there was a wedding in Cana of Galilee, and the mother of Jesus was there. ² Now both Jesus and His disciples were invited to the wedding. ³ And when they ran out of wine, the mother of Jesus said to Him, "They have no wine."

⁴ Jesus said to her, "Woman, what does your concern have to do with Me? My hour has not yet come."

⁵ His mother said to the servants, "Whatever He says to you, do it."

⁶ Now there were set there six waterpots of stone, according to the manner of purification of the Jews, containing twenty or thirty gallons apiece. ⁷ Jesus said to them, "Fill the waterpots with water." And they filled them up to the brim. ⁸ And He said to them, "Draw some out now, and take it to the master of the feast." And they took it. ⁹ When the master of the feast had tasted the water that was made wine, and did not know where it came from (but the servants who had drawn the water knew), the

master of the feast called the bridegroom. ¹⁰ And he said to him, "Every man at the beginning sets out the good wine, and when the guests have well drunk, then the inferior. You have kept the good wine until now!"

¹¹ This beginning of signs Jesus did in Cana of Galilee, and manifested His glory; and His disciples believed in Him.

EXPLORATION

1. Does it seem unusual to you that Jesus would attend a wedding? Why or why not?

_____

_____

_____

_____

2. Why do you think Jesus chose to attend this particular wedding?

_____

_____

_____

3. What did Jesus mean when he said to his mother, "My hour has not yet come" (verse 4)?

_____

_____

_____

4. How did Mary respond to Jesus' reluctance? Why do you think Jesus chose to go ahead and perform this miracle for the guests?

_____

_____

5. Why do you think John adds the detail that the master of the banquet said to the bridegroom, "You have saved the best [wine] till now" (verse 10)?

_____

_____

_____

6. According to verse 11, for whose benefit did Jesus do this miracle?

_____

_____

_____

INSPIRATION

Life is a gift, albeit unassembled. It comes in pieces, and sometimes it falls to pieces. Part A doesn't always fit with part B. The struggle is too great for the strength. Inevitably, something seems to be missing. The pieces of life don't fit. When they don't, take your problem to Jesus.

Mary, the mother of Jesus, did. "On the third day a wedding took place at Cana in Galilee. Jesus' mother was there, and Jesus and his disciples had also been invited to the wedding. When the wine was gone, Jesus' mother said to him, 'They have no more wine'" (John 2:1–3). . . .

Mary wasn't bossy. She didn't say, "Jesus, they are out of wine, so here is what I need you to do. Go down to the grove at the corner, accelerate the growth of some Bordeaux grapes, and turn them into wine." She didn't try to fix the problem herself.

She wasn't critical. "If only they had planned better, Jesus. People just don't think ahead. What is society coming to? The world is going over the cliff! Help, Jesus, help!" She didn't blame the host.

She didn't blame Jesus. "What kind of Messiah are you? If you truly were in control, this never would have happened!"

Nor did she blame herself. "It's all my fault, Jesus. Punish me. I failed as a friend. Now the wedding is ruined. The marriage will collapse. I am to blame."

None of this. Mary didn't whine about the wine. She just stated the problem.

Then "Jesus said to her, 'Woman, what does your concern have to do with Me? My hour has not yet come.' His mother said to the servants, 'Whatever He says to you, do it'" (verses 4–5 NKJV). Originally, Jesus had no intention of saving the wedding banquet. This wasn't the manner or place he had planned to reveal his power. But then Mary entered the story—Mary, someone he loved—with a genuine need.

In my imagination I see Mary turn and walk away. Her face is serene. Her eyes reflect calm. She is untroubled. She has done everything she was supposed to do. She has identified the problem, brought it to Jesus, and left it with him. She trusted him completely. She told the servants, "Whatever he says is okay with me."

In my imagination I see Jesus smile. I hear him chuckle. He looks up into the heavens for a moment and then looks at a cluster of six waterpots over in the corner. . . . At Jesus' command H_2O became abundant merlot. Quick calculation reveals the amount: 908 bottles of wine! The couple could have begun a wine business in Napa Valley.

Problem presented. Prayer answered. Crisis avoided. All because Mary entrusted the problem to Jesus. (From *Before Amen* by Max Lucado.)

REACTION

7. How did Mary demonstrate her complete trust in Jesus?

_____

_____

_____

8. What can you learn from Mary's example as it relates to bringing your problems to God?

_____

_____

_____

9. What tends to prevents people from seeing God's abundant provision in their lives?

_____

_____

_____

10. What are some ways that Jesus has abundantly met your needs in the past?

_____

_____

_____

11. How does remembering God's provision in the past encourage you to trust him with your present needs?

_____

_____

_____

12. How do you think your Christian witness is affected when you don't take time to enjoy life like Jesus did in this story?

_____

_____

_____

LIFE LESSONS

What better way to start our examination of the Son of God than to witness his participation in the highs and lows of daily living! Before we give real attention to the ways Jesus wants to transform our lives, we must reach a better understanding of his complete familiarity with our lives. He's comfortable with us. He knows us intimately—even those things no one else knows. When we come to him with our needs, when we realize that we can bring our emptiness to him, we're finally in a place where we can see his power at work in us.

DEVOTION

Lord Jesus, teach us to appreciate the simple pleasures in life and to enjoy the company of other people. When we have needs, remind us to always bring them to you first—and then trust you to bring the answer. Walk with us today, sharing life's pure pleasures and letting your light fall on life's common way.

JOURNALING

What are some problems that you need to leave with Jesus—and trust him for the answer?

_____

_____

_____

_____

_____

_____

_____

_____

_____

_____

_____

FOR FURTHER READING

To complete the book of John during this twelve-part study, read John 1:35–2:25. For more Bible passages on trusting in God, read Joshua 1:9; Proverbs 3:5; Psalm 37:4–6; Isaiah 41:13; Matthew 6:25; Romans 8:28; and Philippians 4:6.

THE WOMAN AT THE WELL

"Everyone who drinks this water will be thirsty again, but whoever drinks the water I give them will never thirst. Indeed, the water I give them will become in them a spring of water welling up to eternal life."
JOHN 4:13–14

REFLECTION

Some of us can hardly remember a time when we weren't Christians. Others among us have become followers of Jesus more recently. Think about the story of your conversion. How did your life change when you accepted Christ as your Savior?

_____

_____

_____

_____

_____

_____

SITUATION

The shortest route between Jerusalem in the south and Galilee in the north required walking through Samaria. For Jews in Jesus' day, this region was definitely on the "wrong side of the tracks." The Jews despised the Samaritans, and the Samaritans did their best to return the compliment. Jesus often seemed to go out of his way to challenge these traditional animosities. On one occasion, he showed up at the well of Sychar in Samaria just as a woman arrived.

OBSERVATION

*Read John 4:5–30 from the New International
Version or the New King James Version.*

New International Version
⁵ So he came to a town in Samaria called Sychar, near the plot of ground Jacob had given to his son Joseph. ⁶ Jacob's well was there, and Jesus, tired as he was from the journey, sat down by the well. It was about noon.

[7] When a Samaritan woman came to draw water, Jesus said to her, "Will you give me a drink?" [8] (His disciples had gone into the town to buy food.)

[9] The Samaritan woman said to him, "You are a Jew and I am a Samaritan woman. How can you ask me for a drink?" (For Jews do not associate with Samaritans.)

[10] Jesus answered her, "If you knew the gift of God and who it is that asks you for a drink, you would have asked him and he would have given you living water."

[11] "Sir," the woman said, "you have nothing to draw with and the well is deep. Where can you get this living water? [12] Are you greater than our father Jacob, who gave us the well and drank from it himself, as did also his sons and his livestock?"

[13] Jesus answered, "Everyone who drinks this water will be thirsty again, [14] but whoever drinks the water I give them will never thirst. Indeed, the water I give them will become in them a spring of water welling up to eternal life."

[15] The woman said to him, "Sir, give me this water so that I won't get thirsty and have to keep coming here to draw water."

[16] He told her, "Go, call your husband and come back."

[17] "I have no husband," she replied.

Jesus said to her, "You are right when you say you have no husband. [18] The fact is, you have had five husbands, and the man you now have is not your husband. What you have just said is quite true."

[19] "Sir," the woman said, "I can see that you are a prophet. [20] Our ancestors worshiped on this mountain, but you Jews claim that the place where we must worship is in Jerusalem."

[21] "Woman," Jesus replied, "believe me, a time is coming when you will worship the Father neither on this mountain nor in Jerusalem. [22] You Samaritans worship what you do not know; we worship what we do know, for salvation is from the Jews. [23] Yet a time is coming and has now come when the true worshipers will worship the Father in the Spirit and in truth, for they are the kind of worshipers the Father seeks. [24] God is spirit, and his worshipers must worship in the Spirit and in truth."

²⁵ The woman said, "I know that Messiah" (called Christ) "is coming. When he comes, he will explain everything to us."

²⁶ Then Jesus declared, "I, the one speaking to you—I am he."

²⁷ Just then his disciples returned and were surprised to find him talking with a woman. But no one asked, "What do you want?" or "Why are you talking with her?"

²⁸ Then, leaving her water jar, the woman went back to the town and said to the people, ²⁹ "Come, see a man who told me everything I ever did. Could this be the Messiah?" ³⁰ They came out of the town and made their way toward him.

New King James Version

⁵ So He came to a city of Samaria which is called Sychar, near the plot of ground that Jacob gave to his son Joseph. ⁶ Now Jacob's well was there. Jesus therefore, being wearied from His journey, sat thus by the well. It was about the sixth hour.

⁷ A woman of Samaria came to draw water. Jesus said to her, "Give Me a drink." ⁸ For His disciples had gone away into the city to buy food.

⁹ Then the woman of Samaria said to Him, "How is it that You, being a Jew, ask a drink from me, a Samaritan woman?" For Jews have no dealings with Samaritans.

¹⁰ Jesus answered and said to her, "If you knew the gift of God, and who it is who says to you, 'Give Me a drink,' you would have asked Him, and He would have given you living water."

¹¹ The woman said to Him, "Sir, You have nothing to draw with, and the well is deep. Where then do You get that living water? ¹² Are You greater than our father Jacob, who gave us the well, and drank from it himself, as well as his sons and his livestock?"

¹³ Jesus answered and said to her, "Whoever drinks of this water will thirst again, ¹⁴ but whoever drinks of the water that I shall give him will never thirst. But the water that I shall give him will become in him a fountain of water springing up into everlasting life."

¹⁵ The woman said to Him, "Sir, give me this water, that I may not thirst, nor come here to draw."

[16] Jesus said to her, "Go, call your husband, and come here."

[17] The woman answered and said, "I have no husband."

Jesus said to her, "You have well said, 'I have no husband,' [18] for you have had five husbands, and the one whom you now have is not your husband; in that you spoke truly."

[19] The woman said to Him, "Sir, I perceive that You are a prophet. [20] Our fathers worshiped on this mountain, and you Jews say that in Jerusalem is the place where one ought to worship."

[21] Jesus said to her, "Woman, believe Me, the hour is coming when you will neither on this mountain, nor in Jerusalem, worship the Father. [22] You worship what you do not know; we know what we worship, for salvation is of the Jews. [23] But the hour is coming, and now is, when the true worshipers will worship the Father in spirit and truth; for the Father is seeking such to worship Him. [24] God is Spirit, and those who worship Him must worship in spirit and truth."

[25] The woman said to Him, "I know that Messiah is coming" (who is called Christ). "When He comes, He will tell us all things."

[26] Jesus said to her, "I who speak to you am He."

[27] And at this point His disciples came, and they marveled that He talked with a woman; yet no one said, "What do You seek?" or, "Why are You talking with her?"

[28] The woman then left her waterpot, went her way into the city, and said to the men, [29] "Come, see a Man who told me all things that I ever did. Could this be the Christ?" [30] Then they went out of the city and came to Him.

EXPLORATION

1. How did the woman respond when Jesus first spoke to her? Why did she react this way?

_____

_____

_____

2. What did Jesus mean when he said he could give her "living water" (verse 10)?

_____

_____

_____

_____

3. What can you conclude from Jesus' statements about this woman's character?

_____

_____

_____

_____

4. How did Jesus demonstrate his love for this woman in spite of her character?

_____

_____

_____

_____

5. How did the woman react at the end of her encounter with Jesus?

_____

_____

_____

6. What do the woman's actions reveal about the way Jesus affected her life?

_____

_____

_____

INSPIRATION

Talk about a woman who could make a list. Number one, discrimination. She is a Samaritan, hated by Jews. Number two, gender bias. She is a female, condescended to by the men. Third, she is a divorcée, not once, not twice. Let's see if we can count. Four? Five? Five marriages turned south, and now she's sharing a bed with a guy who won't give her a ring.

When I add this up, I envision a happy-hour stool sitter who lives with her mad at half boil. Husky voice, cigarette breath, and a dress cut low at the top and high at the bottom. Certainly not Samaria's finest. Certainly not the woman you'd put in charge of the Ladies' Bible Class.

Which makes the fact that Jesus does just that all the more surprising. He doesn't just put her in charge of the class; he puts her in charge of evangelizing the whole town. Before the day is over, the entire city hears about a man who claims to be God. "He told me everything I ever did" (John 4:39), she tells them, leaving unsaid the obvious, "and he loved me anyway."

A little rain can straighten a flower stem. A little love can change a life. Who knew the last time this woman had been entrusted with anything, much less the biggest news in history! In fact, flip to the left out of John 4, and you'll make this startling discovery. She is Jesus' missionary! She precedes the more noted. The lineage of Peter and Paul, St. Patrick and St. Francis of Assisi can be traced back to a town trollop who was so overwhelmed by Christ that she had to speak. . . .

Why? Not just because of what Jesus did, though that was huge. But because she let him do it. She let him on board. She let him love her. (From *A Love Worth Giving* by Max Lucado.)

REACTION

7. In what ways can you identify with the woman in this story?

8. What does this story reveal about God's attitude toward sinful people?

_____

_____

_____

9. When have you felt God's concern and love for you?

_____

_____

_____

10. How does the woman's response to Jesus inspire you?

_____

_____

_____

11. How do Jesus' actions in this story encourage you to treat others?

_____

_____

_____

12. How are you showing God's love to others in your life?

_____

_____

_____

LIFE LESSONS

When we least expect Jesus in our lives, he shows up. Sometimes, when we are actively trying to avoid anything that would remind us that our lives are not as they should be, we find Jesus waiting in the very place we have run to hide. Jesus never forces himself on us, but he does have an uncanny way of interrupting our thoughts and actions with truthful questions and challenging ideas. Just think about the times Jesus has showed up in your life as a way of starting a life-changing episode with you.

DEVOTION

Father, your Word assures us that no one is beyond hope. You accept and love each one of us, in spite of our failures. You offer us salvation. You offer us mercy. You offer us love. Thank you for intervening in our lives and rescuing us from the bondage of sin. We praise you for your mercy, forgiveness, and love.

JOURNALING

How can you reach out to others as Jesus did?

FOR FURTHER READING

To complete the book of John during this twelve-part study, read John 3:1–4:42. For more Bible passages on God's mercy and love for sinners, read Exodus 34:6; Deuteronomy 4:31; Luke 19:1–10; John 3:16; 8:3–11; and Ephesians 2:1–6.

LESSON FOUR

HEALING THE SICK

When Jesus saw him lying there, and knew that he already had been in that condition a long time, He said to him, "Do you want to be made well?"
JOHN 5:6 NKJV

REFLECTION

There are many hurting people in our society—the poor, the sick, the homeless, the incarcerated. There are people with inner wounds—the grieving, the lonely, the depressed. All too often they are not only forgotten but also invisible. Think about the people in your sphere of influence. How can you take notice? Who can you help and support this week?

SITUATION

Throughout the year, the Jewish people would gather in Jerusalem. Most of the people came to attend the three major feasts. Some came on healing pilgrimages, expecting to find wholeness in the city of David. One particular man came to bathe in the waters of the pool of Bethesda, which was said to provide healing when an angel stirred the water. But even though the man had spent years near the pool, he was unable to get past the others in need of healing when the waters were stirred. Jesus took time out from his Sabbath to speak to this man.

OBSERVATION

Read John 5:1–15 from the New International Version or the New King James Version.

NEW INTERNATIONAL VERSION

[1] Some time later, Jesus went up to Jerusalem for one of the Jewish festivals. [2] Now there is in Jerusalem near the Sheep Gate a pool, which in Aramaic is called Bethesda and which is surrounded by five covered

colonnades. ³ Here a great number of disabled people used to lie—the blind, the lame, the paralyzed. [4] ⁵ One who was there had been an invalid for thirty-eight years.

⁶ When Jesus saw him lying there and learned that he had been in this condition for a long time, he asked him, "Do you want to get well?"

⁷ "Sir," the invalid replied, "I have no one to help me into the pool when the water is stirred. While I am trying to get in, someone else goes down ahead of me."

⁸ Then Jesus said to him, "Get up! Pick up your mat and walk." ⁹ At once the man was cured; he picked up his mat and walked.

The day on which this took place was a Sabbath, ¹⁰ and so the Jewish leaders said to the man who had been healed, "It is the Sabbath; the law forbids you to carry your mat."

¹¹ But he replied, "The man who made me well said to me, 'Pick up your mat and walk.'"

¹² So they asked him, "Who is this fellow who told you to pick it up and walk?"

¹³ The man who was healed had no idea who it was, for Jesus had slipped away into the crowd that was there.

¹⁴ Later Jesus found him at the temple and said to him, "See, you are well again. Stop sinning or something worse may happen to you." ¹⁵ The man went away and told the Jewish leaders that it was Jesus who had made him well.

New King James Version

¹ After this there was a feast of the Jews, and Jesus went up to Jerusalem. ² Now there is in Jerusalem by the Sheep Gate a pool, which is called in Hebrew, Bethesda, having five porches. ³ In these lay a great multitude of sick people, blind, lame, paralyzed, waiting for the moving of the water. ⁴ For an angel went down at a certain time into the pool and stirred up the water; then whoever stepped in first, after the stirring of the water, was made well of whatever disease he had. ⁵ Now a certain man was there who had an infirmity thirty-eight years. ⁶ When Jesus saw him

lying there, and knew that he already had been in that condition a long time, He said to him, "Do you want to be made well?"

⁷ The sick man answered Him, "Sir, I have no man to put me into the pool when the water is stirred up; but while I am coming, another steps down before me."

⁸ Jesus said to him, "Rise, take up your bed and walk." ⁹ And immediately the man was made well, took up his bed, and walked.

And that day was the Sabbath. ¹⁰ The Jews therefore said to him who was cured, "It is the Sabbath; it is not lawful for you to carry your bed."

¹¹ He answered them, "He who made me well said to me, 'Take up your bed and walk.'"

¹² Then they asked him, "Who is the Man who said to you, 'Take up your bed and walk'?" ¹³ But the one who was healed did not know who it was, for Jesus had withdrawn, a multitude being in that place. ¹⁴ Afterward Jesus found him in the temple, and said to him, "See, you have been made well. Sin no more, lest a worse thing come upon you."

¹⁵ The man departed and told the Jews that it was Jesus who had made him well.

EXPLORATION

1. What do you think motivated Jesus to go to Bethesda during a time of celebration?

_____

_____

_____

_____

2. How would you describe the life of the invalid man in this story?

_____

_____

_____

_____

3. Why do you think Jesus chose to help this particular man?

_____

_____

_____

4. Why do you think the religious leaders reacted to the man's healing in the way they did?

_____

_____

_____

5. What does the response of the religious leaders reveal about their hearts and motives?

_____

_____

_____

6. Why was it important to Jesus to speak to the man again after healing him?

_____

_____

_____

INSPIRATION

It's called Bethesda. It could be called Central Park, Metropolitan Hospital, or even Joe's Bar and Grill. It could be the homeless huddled beneath a downtown overpass. It could be Calvary Baptist. It could be any collection of hurting people.

An underwater spring caused the pool to bubble occasionally. The people believed the bubbles were caused by the dipping of angels' wings. They also believed that the first person to touch the water after the angel did would be healed. Did healing occur? I don't know. But I do know crowds of invalids came to give it a try.

Picture a battleground strewn with wounded bodies, and you see Bethesda. Imagine a nursing home overcrowded and understaffed, and you see the pool. Call to mind the orphans in Bangladesh or the abandoned in New Delhi, and you will see what people saw when they passed Bethesda. As they passed, what did they hear? An endless wave of groans. What did they witness? A field of faceless need. What did they do? Most walked past, ignoring the people.

But not Jesus. He is in Jerusalem for a feast. . . . He is alone. He is not there to teach the disciples or to draw a crowd. The people need him—so he's there.

Can you picture it? Jesus walking among the suffering.

What is he thinking? When an infected hand touches his ankle, what does he do? When a blind child stumbles in Jesus' path, does he reach down to catch the child? When a wrinkled hand extends for alms, how does Jesus respond?

Whether the watering hole is Bethesda or Bill's Bar . . . how does God feel when people hurt?

It's worth the telling of the story if all we do is watch him walk. It's worth it just to know he even came. He didn't have to, you know. Surely there are more sanitary crowds in Jerusalem. Surely there are more enjoyable activities. After all, this is the Passover feast. It's an exciting time in the holy city. People have come from miles around to meet God in the temple.

Little do they know that God is with the sick.

Little do they know that God is walking slowly, stepping carefully between the beggars and the blind.

Little do they know that the strong young carpenter who surveys the ragged landscape of pain is God. (From *He Still Moves Stones* by Max Lucado.)

REACTION

7. How were others affected who witnessed the healing of the invalid man?

_____

_____

_____

8. What are some of the challenges of ministering to people with a serious illness? What are some of the rewards?

_____

_____

_____

9. How can you demonstrate God's love to people who are suffering?

_____

_____

_____

10. How can you become more sensitive to the suffering of others?

_____

_____

_____

11. What does this story reveal about why it is important for believers to minister to hurting people?

_____

_____

_____

12. Do you know someone who is hurting? How can you reach out to that person?

_____

_____

_____

LIFE LESSONS

Jesus went to places where people were hurting. There was intention in his steps. We can claim there are hurting people all around us, but if we are going to live by Jesus' example, we need to make it part of our lifestyle to visit places where people are obviously hurting: prisons, hospitals, disaster areas, nursing homes—the list is pretty obvious. We may not know how we can help, but we will never find that out or discover how God can use us if we avoid the company of suffering people.

DEVOTION

Forgive us, Father, for any time we have ignored the needs of others. Help us respond to the suffering around us. Fill us with your love. Give us your compassion for the hurting, your love for the despised, and your mercy for the afflicted.

JOURNALING

How have you felt God's love for you during painful times?

_____

_____

_____

_____

_____

_____

_____

_____

_____

_____

FOR FURTHER READING

To complete the book of John during this twelve-part study, read John 4:43–5:47. For more Bible passages about helping the needy, read Matthew 25:34–46; 1 Thessalonians 5:14; and Hebrews 6:10–11.

A HUNGRY CROWD

When they had all had enough to eat, he said to his disciples,
"Gather the pieces that are left over. Let nothing be wasted."
So they gathered them and filled twelve baskets with the pieces
of the five barley loaves left over by those who had eaten.

JOHN 6:12–13

REFLECTION

At first glance, the need often looks greater than the resources. We might think what we have been given to accomplish the task is insufficient—until we place them in the hands of someone who knows what to do with them. God can often take a little gift and make something great out of it. Think of a time when God provided for your needs in an unusual or surprising way. How did that experience strengthen your faith?

_____

_____

_____

_____

_____

SITUATION

We live in a world of fast-food restaurants and readily available sources of food. We can hardly imagine a crowd of several thousand, hungry and without relief. They have been receiving "spiritual" food in the form of teaching from Jesus throughout the day, but now their physical needs are beginning to distract them. Jesus takes this opportunity to offer his followers a valuable lesson.

OBSERVATION

Read John 6:1–15 from the New International Version or the New King James Version.

NEW INTERNATIONAL VERSION

[1] Some time after this, Jesus crossed to the far shore of the Sea of Galilee (that is, the Sea of Tiberias), [2] and a great crowd of people followed him because they saw the signs he had performed by healing the sick. [3] Then

Jesus went up on a mountainside and sat down with his disciples. ⁴ The Jewish Passover Festival was near.

⁵ When Jesus looked up and saw a great crowd coming toward him, he said to Philip, "Where shall we buy bread for these people to eat?" ⁶ He asked this only to test him, for he already had in mind what he was going to do.

⁷ Philip answered him, "It would take more than half a year's wages to buy enough bread for each one to have a bite!"

⁸ Another of his disciples, Andrew, Simon Peter's brother, spoke up, ⁹ "Here is a boy with five small barley loaves and two small fish, but how far will they go among so many?"

¹⁰ Jesus said, "Have the people sit down." There was plenty of grass in that place, and they sat down (about five thousand men were there). ¹¹ Jesus then took the loaves, gave thanks, and distributed to those who were seated as much as they wanted. He did the same with the fish.

¹² When they had all had enough to eat, he said to his disciples, "Gather the pieces that are left over. Let nothing be wasted." ¹³ So they gathered them and filled twelve baskets with the pieces of the five barley loaves left over by those who had eaten.

¹⁴ After the people saw the sign Jesus performed, they began to say, "Surely this is the Prophet who is to come into the world." ¹⁵ Jesus, knowing that they intended to come and make him king by force, withdrew again to a mountain by himself.

New King James Version

¹ After these things Jesus went over the Sea of Galilee, which is the Sea of Tiberias. ² Then a great multitude followed Him, because they saw His signs which He performed on those who were diseased. ³ And Jesus went up on the mountain, and there He sat with His disciples.

⁴ Now the Passover, a feast of the Jews, was near. ⁵ Then Jesus lifted up His eyes, and seeing a great multitude coming toward Him, He said to Philip, "Where shall we buy bread, that these may eat?" ⁶ But this He said to test him, for He Himself knew what He would do.

[7] Philip answered Him, "Two hundred denarii worth of bread is not sufficient for them, that every one of them may have a little."

[8] One of His disciples, Andrew, Simon Peter's brother, said to Him, [9] "There is a lad here who has five barley loaves and two small fish, but what are they among so many?"

[10] Then Jesus said, "Make the people sit down." Now there was much grass in the place. So the men sat down, in number about five thousand. [11] And Jesus took the loaves, and when He had given thanks He distributed them to the disciples, and the disciples to those sitting down; and likewise of the fish, as much as they wanted. [12] So when they were filled, He said to His disciples, "Gather up the fragments that remain, so that nothing is lost." [13] Therefore they gathered them up, and filled twelve baskets with the fragments of the five barley loaves which were left over by those who had eaten. [14] Then those men, when they had seen the sign that Jesus did, said, "This is truly the Prophet who is to come into the world."

[15] Therefore when Jesus perceived that they were about to come and take Him by force to make Him king, He departed again to the mountain by Himself alone.

EXPLORATION

1. Why do you think the people went out to see Jesus without bringing along any food? (This event is also described in Matthew 14:13–21; Mark 6:30–44; and Luke 9:10–17.)

_____

_____

_____

2. Why did Jesus ask Philip how they could feed the crowd?

_____

_____

_____

3. What can we learn from Philip's response? What was the larger obstacle for Philip: the lack of food or the costs involved in feeding such a large crowd?

4. What do you think was Jesus' purpose in having the disciples gather up the leftovers?

5. What did Jesus want his disciples to learn from this event?

6. Who are you most like in this story? Philip? Andrew? The boy? The people? Why?

INSPIRATION

Interestingly, the stress seen that day is not on Jesus' face, but on the faces of the disciples. "Send the crowds away," they demand. Fair request. "After all," they are saying, "You've taught them. You've healed them. You've accommodated them. And now they're getting hungry. If we don't send them away, they'll want you to feed them, too!"

I wish I could have seen the expression on the disciples' faces when they heard the Master's response. . . .

"You give them something to eat." . . .

Rather than look to God, they looked in their wallets. "That would take eight months of a man's wages! Are we to go and spend that much on bread and give it to them to eat?"

"Y-y-y-you've got to be kidding." "He can't be serious."

"It's one of Jesus' jokes."

"Do you know how many people are out there?"

Eyes watermelon wide. Jaws dangling open. One ear hearing the din of the crowd, the other the command of God.

Don't miss the contrasting views. When Jesus saw the people, he saw an opportunity to love and affirm value. When the disciples saw the people they saw thousands of problems.

Also, don't miss the irony. In the midst of a bakery—in the presence of the Eternal Baker—they tell the "Bread of Life" that there is no bread.

How silly we must appear to God.

Here's where Jesus should have given up. This is the point in the pressure-packed day where Jesus should have exploded. The sorrow, the life threats, the exuberance, the crowds, the interruptions, the demands, and now this. His own disciples can't do what he asks them. In front of five thousand men, they let him down.

"Beam me up, Father," should have been Jesus' next words. But they weren't. Instead he inquires, "How many loaves do you have?"

The disciples bring him a little boy's lunch. A lunch pail becomes a banquet, and all are fed. No word of reprimand is given. No furrowed brow of anger is seen. No "I-told-you-so" speech is delivered. The same compassion Jesus extends to the crowd is extended to his friends. (From *In the Eye of the Storm* by Max Lucado.)

REACTION

7. What problems in your life seem to have no solutions?

_____

_____

_____

8. Do you find it difficult to trust God to meet your needs? Why?

9. What does this story teach about the way God provides for his people?

10. In what ways has God given you wisdom and strength to overcome difficulties in your life?

11. Based on this event, how do you think God wants you to deal with your doubts?

12. How does the faith of other believers inspire you to trust God?

LIFE LESSONS

It's never about how much we have to offer, but rather if we will offer whatever we have. Jesus had the power to create food out of thin air or from the rocks on the hillside, but he chose to work with a small gift from a little boy. Sometimes, the greatest miracle happens when we let go of some little possession and put it into God's hands. What God does with what we give him becomes secondary to the delight of participating in his work in the world.

DEVOTION

Father, why do we doubt you? Time and again you have proved your faithfulness, yet our faith falters. Thank you for continually providing for our needs. Keep us from doubt. Fill us with faith in you. Remind us that you are bigger than all of our problems and needs.

JOURNALING

What keeps you from completely trusting in God to meet your needs?

_____

_____

_____

_____

_____

_____

_____

_____

_____

_____

FOR FURTHER READING

To complete the book of John during this twelve-part study, read John 6:1–71. For more Bible passages on God's provision for his people, read Genesis 2:15–16; Exodus 16:1–31; Psalm 20:7; Proverbs 3:5–10; and Matthew 6:25–34.

A GUILTY WOMAN

So when they continued asking Him, He raised Himself up and said to them, "He who is without sin among you, let him throw a stone at her first."
JOHN 8:7 NKJV

REFLECTION

The longing for love and acceptance that makes us human can also lead us to make shameful and sad choices. Even more shocking are some of the thoughtless and evil acts people commit toward others they deem less worthy of love. Yet each of us desires those marvelous moments when we feel valued and appreciated by someone else. What are some responses or gestures that make you feel loved and accepted by others?

_____

_____

_____

_____

SITUATION

John includes a brief episode in his Gospel to illustrate the lengths some people were willing to go in order to trap and destroy Jesus. Certain leaders had already attempted to undermine his position, and efforts had been made to arrest him. These leaders continued to test Jesus' orthodoxy with a crude confrontation in which a woman, clearly guilty of an offense, was brought before him. They had little interest in justice. They simply asked Jesus, "What do you say?" Neither the opponents nor the woman expected the answer Jesus gave.

OBSERVATION

Read John 8:1–11 from the New International
Version or the New King James Version.

NEW INTERNATIONAL VERSION
[1] But Jesus went to the Mount of Olives. [2] At dawn he appeared again in the temple courts, where all the people gathered around him, and

he sat down to teach them. ³ The teachers of the law and the Pharisees brought in a woman caught in adultery. They made her stand before the group ⁴ and said to Jesus, "Teacher, this woman was caught in the act of adultery. ⁵ In the Law Moses commanded us to stone such women. Now what do you say?" ⁶ They were using this question as a trap, in order to have a basis for accusing him.

But Jesus bent down and started to write on the ground with his finger. ⁷ When they kept on questioning him, he straightened up and said to them, "Let any one of you who is without sin be the first to throw a stone at her." ⁸ Again he stooped down and wrote on the ground.

⁹ At this, those who heard began to go away one at a time, the older ones first, until only Jesus was left, with the woman still standing there. ¹⁰ Jesus straightened up and asked her, "Woman, where are they? Has no one condemned you?"

¹¹ "No one, sir," she said.

"Then neither do I condemn you," Jesus declared. "Go now and leave your life of sin."

New King James Version

¹ But Jesus went to the Mount of Olives. ² Now early in the morning He came again into the temple, and all the people came to Him; and He sat down and taught them. ³ Then the scribes and Pharisees brought to Him a woman caught in adultery. And when they had set her in the midst, ⁴ they said to Him, "Teacher, this woman was caught in adultery, in the very act. ⁵ Now Moses, in the law, commanded us that such should be stoned. But what do You say?" ⁶ This they said, testing Him, that they might have something of which to accuse Him. But Jesus stooped down and wrote on the ground with His finger, as though He did not hear.

⁷ So when they continued asking Him, He raised Himself up and said to them, "He who is without sin among you, let him throw a stone at her first." ⁸ And again He stooped down and wrote on the ground. ⁹ Then those who heard it, being convicted by their conscience, went out one by one, beginning with the oldest even to the last. And Jesus was left alone,

and the woman standing in the midst. ¹⁰ When Jesus had raised Himself up and saw no one but the woman, He said to her, "Woman, where are those accusers of yours? Has no one condemned you?"

¹¹ She said, "No one, Lord."

And Jesus said to her, "Neither do I condemn you; go and sin no more."

EXPLORATION

1. Why did the religious leaders bring the adulterous woman to Jesus? (See Leviticus 20:10 and Deuteronomy 22:22 for the Old Testament background of their charges.)

_____

_____

_____

2. Why did the religious leaders ask Jesus what they should do with the woman?

_____

_____

_____

3. How was Jesus' attitude toward the woman different from the crowd's attitude?

_____

_____

_____

4. Why do you think the older men were the first to leave the scene?

_____

_____

_____

5. With which group or person in the story do you identify the most?

_____

_____

_____

6. What words would you use to describe the way Jesus treated the guilty woman? How did he address her sin?

_____

_____

_____

INSPIRATION

Sightless and heartless redeemers. Redeemers without power. That's not the Redeemer of the New Testament.

Jesus sits surrounded by a horseshoe of listeners. Some nod their heads in agreement and open their hearts in obedience. They have accepted the teacher as their teacher and are learning to accept him as their Lord.

We don't know his topic that morning. Prayer, perhaps. Or maybe kindness or anxiety. But whatever it was, it was soon interrupted when people burst into the courtyard.

Determined, they erupt out of a narrow street and stomp toward Jesus. The listeners scramble to get out of the way. The mob is made up of religious leaders, the elders and deacons of their day. Respected and important men. And struggling to keep her balance on the crest of this angry wave is a scantily clad woman.

Only moments before she had been in bed with a man who was not her husband. Was this how she made her living? Maybe. Maybe not. We don't know.

But we do know that a door was jerked open and she was yanked from a bed. She barely had time to cover her body before she was dragged into the street by two men the age of her father.

And now, with holy strides, the mob storms toward the teacher. They throw the woman in his direction. She nearly falls.

"We found this woman in bed with a man!" cries the leader. "The law says to stone her. What do you say?"

In her despair she looks at the Teacher. His eyes don't glare. "Don't worry," they whisper, "it's okay." And for the first time that morning she sees kindness.

As Jesus looked at this daughter, did his mind race back? Did he relive the act of forming this child in heaven? Did he see her as he had originally made her?

So, with the tenderness only a father can have, he set out to untie the knots and repair the holes.

He begins by diverting the crowd's attention. He draws on the ground. Everybody looks down. The woman feels relief as the eyes of the men look away from her.

The accusers are persistent. "Tell us, teacher! What do you want us to do with her?"

He just raised his head and offered an invitation, "I guess if you've never made a mistake, then you have a right to stone this woman." He looked back down and began to draw on the earth again.

Someone cleared his throat as if to speak, but no one spoke. Feet shuffled. Eyes dropped. Then thud ... thud ... thud ... rocks fell to the ground.

And they walked away. They came as one, but they left one by one. Jesus told the woman to look up. "Is there no one to condemn you?"

Maybe she expected him to scold her. Perhaps she expected him to walk away from her. I'm not sure, but I do know this: What she got, she never expected. She got a promise and a commission.

The promise: "Then neither do I condemn you." The commission: "Go and sin no more."

The woman turns and walks into anonymity. She's never seen or heard from again. But we can be confident of one thing: On that morning in Jerusalem, she saw Jesus and Jesus saw her. And could we somehow transport her to Rio de Janeiro and let her stand at the base of the *Cristo Redentor*, I know what her response would be.

"That's not the Jesus I saw," she would say. For the Jesus she saw didn't have a hard heart. And the Jesus that saw her didn't have blind eyes.

However, if we could somehow transport her to Calvary and let her stand at the base of the cross . . . you know what she would say. "That's him."

She would recognize his voice. It's raspier and weaker, but the words are the same, "Father, forgive them . . ." And she would recognize his eyes. How could she ever forget those eyes? Clear and tear-filled. Eyes that saw her not as she was, but as she was intended to be. (From *Six Hours One Friday* by Max Lucado.)

REACTION

7. How does Jesus' interaction with this sinful woman encourage you?

_____

_____

_____

_____

8. What was the attitude of the religious leaders toward the woman? Toward Jesus?

_____

_____

_____

_____

9. How can we avoid these same attitudes?

_____

_____

_____

_____

10. What does this passage reveal about God's view of sin?

_____

_____

_____

11. Why do you think we rank some sins as being far worse than others?

_____

_____

_____

12. How does this passage challenge your attitude about people caught in certain sins?

_____

_____

_____

LIFE LESSONS

God loves with an informed passion. Jesus didn't look at the woman caught in adultery as a stranger for whom he could practice mercy. In his look, she met someone who knew exactly who she was and what she had done. And yet, despite his awareness, Jesus did not treat her as an object to make a point or a pawn to manipulate. He spoke the truth—and he set her free to go and sin no more. No matter how often we come to Christ, burdened and fallen again, he is willing to say to us, "Go, and sin no more."

DEVOTION

Father, you are compassionate and forgiving. Like the woman in this story, we stand amazed that you would have such mercy on us. We thank you for your unconditional love. We are not what we should be, but we accept your forgiveness and claim your salvation.

JOURNALING

For what sinful attitudes or actions do you need to ask God's forgiveness?

FOR FURTHER READING

To complete the book of John during this twelve-part study, read John 7:1–8:59. For more Bible passages on God's forgiveness, read Exodus 34:6–7; Deuteronomy 4:31; Luke 1:50; Acts 10:43; Ephesians 1:7; 2:4–5; and 1 John 1:8–9.

LESSON SEVEN

A MAN BORN BLIND

His disciples asked him, "Rabbi, who sinned, this man or his parents, that he was born blind?" "Neither this man nor his parents sinned," said Jesus, "but this happened so that the works of God might be displayed in him.
JOHN 9:2–3

REFLECTION

We all are born with disabilities, whether they are physical, emotional, or spiritual ones. The hard part is admitting this and letting God use them. Think about your personal strengths and weaknesses. How has God worked through your weaknesses for his glory?

_____

_____

_____

_____

_____

SITUATION

As Jesus traveled with his disciples, they came upon a man who had been blind from birth. The encounter sparked a theological question from the disciples, but then quickly escalated into a major confrontation about the rules of the Sabbath. Jesus used the episode to reveal how we develop a distorted view of God when we limit his actions or inflate his commandments.

OBSERVATION

Read John 9:1–12 from the New International Version or the New King James Version.

New International Version

¹ As he went along, he saw a man blind from birth. ² His disciples asked him, "Rabbi, who sinned, this man or his parents, that he was born blind?"

³ "Neither this man nor his parents sinned," said Jesus, "but this happened so that the works of God might be displayed in him. ⁴ As long as it

is day, we must do the works of him who sent me. Night is coming, when no one can work. [5] While I am in the world, I am the light of the world."

[6] After saying this, he spit on the ground, made some mud with the saliva, and put it on the man's eyes. [7] "Go," he told him, "wash in the Pool of Siloam" (this word means "Sent"). So the man went and washed, and came home seeing.

[8] His neighbors and those who had formerly seen him begging asked, "Isn't this the same man who used to sit and beg?" [9] Some claimed that he was.

Others said, "No, he only looks like him."

But he himself insisted, "I am the man."

[10] "How then were your eyes opened?" they asked.

[11] He replied, "The man they call Jesus made some mud and put it on my eyes. He told me to go to Siloam and wash. So I went and washed, and then I could see."

[12] "Where is this man?" they asked him.

"I don't know," he said.

New King James Version

[1] Now as Jesus passed by, He saw a man who was blind from birth. [2] And His disciples asked Him, saying, "Rabbi, who sinned, this man or his parents, that he was born blind?"

[3] Jesus answered, "Neither this man nor his parents sinned, but that the works of God should be revealed in him. [4] I must work the works of Him who sent Me while it is day; the night is coming when no one can work. [5] As long as I am in the world, I am the light of the world."

[6] When He had said these things, He spat on the ground and made clay with the saliva; and He anointed the eyes of the blind man with the clay. [7] And He said to him, "Go, wash in the pool of Siloam" (which is translated, Sent). So he went and washed, and came back seeing.

[8] Therefore the neighbors and those who previously had seen that he was blind said, "Is not this he who sat and begged?"

[9] Some said, "This is he." Others said, "He is like him."

He said, "I am he."

¹⁰ Therefore they said to him, "How were your eyes opened?"

¹¹ He answered and said, "A Man called Jesus made clay and anointed my eyes and said to me, 'Go to the pool of Siloam and wash.' So I went and washed, and I received sight."

¹² Then they said to him, "Where is He?"

He said, "I do not know."

EXPLORATION

1. What assumptions did Jesus' followers make about this man's blindness?

_____

_____

_____

_____

2. How did Jesus correct these misconceptions?

_____

_____

_____

_____

3. What did Jesus mean when he said, "Night is coming, when no one can work" (verse 4)?

_____

_____

_____

_____

4. How did Jesus involve the blind man in the healing process?

_____

_____

_____

_____

5. Why do you think Jesus sent the man to wash in a pool before he healed him?

_____

_____

_____

6. How did the people of the town respond to the miracle?

_____

_____

_____

INSPIRATION

The followers thought the blind man was a great theological case study. "Why do you think he's blind?" one asked. "He must have sinned."

"No, it's his folks' fault."

"Jesus, what do you think? Why is he blind?"

"He's blind to show what God can do."

The apostles knew what was coming; they had seen this look in Jesus' eyes before. They knew what he was going to do, but they didn't know how he was going to do it. *Lightning? Thunder? A shout? A clap of the hands?* They all watched.

Jesus began to work his mouth a little. The onlookers stared. "What is he doing?" He moved his jaw as if he were chewing on something.

Some of the people began to get restless. Jesus just chewed. His jaw rotated around until he had what he wanted. Spit. Ordinary saliva.

If no one said it, somebody had to be thinking it: *yuck!*

Jesus spat on the ground, stuck his finger into the puddle, and stirred. Soon it was a mud pie, and he smeared some of the mud across the blind man's eyes.

The same One who had turned a stick into a scepter and a pebble into a missile now turned saliva and mud into a balm for the blind.

Once again, the mundane became majestic. Once again the dull became divine, the humdrum holy. Once again God's power was seen, not through the ability of the instrument, but through its availability.

"Blessed are the meek," Jesus explained.

Blessed are the available. Blessed are the conduits, the tunnels, the tools. Deliriously joyful are the ones who believe that if God has used sticks, rocks, and spit to do his will, then he can use us. (From *The Applause of Heaven* by Max Lucado.)

REACTION

7. What do you learn from responses of the blind man and the townspeople to Jesus?

_____

_____

_____

8. If you had been one of the townspeople, how do you think you would have responded?

_____

_____

_____

9. When have you seen a person's weakness or disability used for God's glory?

_____

_____

_____

10. What fresh insight have you gained from this passage about the struggles of life?

_____

_____

_____

11. How do you need to change your attitude toward your personal weaknesses and strengths?

_____

_____

_____

_____

_____

12. Why does God choose to use weaknesses and problems to bring glory to himself?

_____

_____

_____

_____

_____

LIFE LESSONS

We find it difficult to trust God when we can't figure out why he allows certain uncomfortable things to happen to us. Interestingly, we don't seem to wonder about God when he allows _good_ things into our lives. One of the life lessons in the blind man's experience is the reminder that no matter how long we've known Christ, we will never get over the fact that he knew us long before we knew him—and that we will never reach the end of discovering more about him.

DEVOTION

We pray, O Father, that you would increase our faith. Forgive us for doubting your ability to use us for your glory. Forgive us for demanding proof instead of simply believing in you. Use all that we have to accomplish your purposes.

JOURNALING

What are some ways God has used your weaknesses or problems for his glory?

_____

_____

_____

_____

_____

_____

_____

_____

_____

_____

_____

_____

_____

_____

_____

_____

_____

_____

_____

_____

FOR FURTHER READING

To complete the book of John during this twelve-part study, read John 9:1–10:42. For more Bible passages on being used by God, read Exodus 3:7–4:12; Joshua 1:1–9; Romans 8:26; 1 Corinthians 1:26–28; 2 Corinthians 12:7–10; and 2 Timothy 2:21.

THE LOSS OF A FRIEND

*"I am the resurrection and the life. He who believes
in Me, though he may die, he shall live. And whoever
lives and believes in Me shall never die."*
JOHN 11:25–26 NKJV

REFLECTION

Losses are never an enjoyable part of life, and losing a friend is particularly sad. God's presence in our lives should cast a slightly different light on losses—especially those caused by death, for even death does not limit God's power. If we can trust him to bring good out of even matters of life and death, can we not learn to trust him with smaller losses? Think of a time in your life when a bad experience turned out for good. How did that affect you?

_____

_____

_____

_____

_____

_____

_____

_____

_____

_____

SITUATION

As Jesus traveled in the region of Perea, located east of the Jordan River, he received word that his friend Lazarus had fallen ill. Lazarus and his sisters, Mary and Martha, were close to Jesus, and he had often stayed in their home. Yet on this occasion, Jesus deliberately delayed in returning back to their home in Bethany. It had already taken time for the messenger to track down Jesus, and now he waited an extra two days. The travel from Perea to Bethany also took time. By the time Jesus arrived, Lazarus had been in the tomb for four days.

OBSERVATION

Read John 11:17–44 from the New International
Version or the New King James Version.

NEW INTERNATIONAL VERSION

[17] On his arrival, Jesus found that Lazarus had already been in the tomb for four days. [18] Now Bethany was less than two miles from Jerusalem, [19] and many Jews had come to Martha and Mary to comfort them in the loss of their brother. [20] When Martha heard that Jesus was coming, she went out to meet him, but Mary stayed at home.

[21] "Lord," Martha said to Jesus, "if you had been here, my brother would not have died. [22] But I know that even now God will give you whatever you ask."

[23] Jesus said to her, "Your brother will rise again."

[24] Martha answered, "I know he will rise again in the resurrection at the last day."

[25] Jesus said to her, "I am the resurrection and the life. The one who believes in me will live, even though they die; [26] and whoever lives by believing in me will never die. Do you believe this?"

[27] "Yes, Lord," she replied, "I believe that you are the Messiah, the Son of God, who is to come into the world."

[28] After she had said this, she went back and called her sister Mary aside. "The Teacher is here," she said, "and is asking for you." [29] When Mary heard this, she got up quickly and went to him. [30] Now Jesus had not yet entered the village, but was still at the place where Martha had met him. [31] When the Jews who had been with Mary in the house, comforting her, noticed how quickly she got up and went out, they followed her, supposing she was going to the tomb to mourn there.

[32] When Mary reached the place where Jesus was and saw him, she fell at his feet and said, "Lord, if you had been here, my brother would not have died."

[33] When Jesus saw her weeping, and the Jews who had come along with her also weeping, he was deeply moved in spirit and troubled. [34] "Where have you laid him?" he asked.

"Come and see, Lord," they replied.

[35] Jesus wept.

[36] Then the Jews said, "See how he loved him!"

[37] But some of them said, "Could not he who opened the eyes of the blind man have kept this man from dying?"

[38] Jesus, once more deeply moved, came to the tomb. It was a cave with a stone laid across the entrance. [39] "Take away the stone," he said.

"But, Lord," said Martha, the sister of the dead man, "by this time there is a bad odor, for he has been there four days."

[40] Then Jesus said, "Did I not tell you that if you believe, you will see the glory of God?"

[41] So they took away the stone. Then Jesus looked up and said, "Father, I thank you that you have heard me. [42] I knew that you always hear me, but I said this for the benefit of the people standing here, that they may believe that you sent me."

[43] When he had said this, Jesus called in a loud voice, "Lazarus, come out!" [44] The dead man came out, his hands and feet wrapped with strips of linen, and a cloth around his face.

Jesus said to them, "Take off the grave clothes and let him go."

New King James Version

[17] So when Jesus came, He found that he had already been in the tomb four days. [18] Now Bethany was near Jerusalem, about two miles away. [19] And many of the Jews had joined the women around Martha and Mary, to comfort them concerning their brother.

[20] Now Martha, as soon as she heard that Jesus was coming, went and met Him, but Mary was sitting in the house. [21] Now Martha said to Jesus, "Lord, if You had been here, my brother would not have died. [22] But even now I know that whatever You ask of God, God will give You."

[23] Jesus said to her, "Your brother will rise again."

[24] Martha said to Him, "I know that he will rise again in the resurrection at the last day."

[25] Jesus said to her, "I am the resurrection and the life. He who believes

in Me, though he may die, he shall live. ²⁶ And whoever lives and believes in Me shall never die. Do you believe this?"

²⁷ She said to Him, "Yes, Lord, I believe that You are the Christ, the Son of God, who is to come into the world."

²⁸ And when she had said these things, she went her way and secretly called Mary her sister, saying, "The Teacher has come and is calling for you." ²⁹ As soon as she heard that, she arose quickly and came to Him. ³⁰ Now Jesus had not yet come into the town, but was in the place where Martha met Him. ³¹ Then the Jews who were with her in the house, and comforting her, when they saw that Mary rose up quickly and went out, followed her, saying, "She is going to the tomb to weep there."

³² Then, when Mary came where Jesus was, and saw Him, she fell down at His feet, saying to Him, "Lord, if You had been here, my brother would not have died."

³³ Therefore, when Jesus saw her weeping, and the Jews who came with her weeping, He groaned in the spirit and was troubled. ³⁴ And He said, "Where have you laid him?"

They said to Him, "Lord, come and see."

³⁵ Jesus wept. ³⁶ Then the Jews said, "See how He loved him!"

³⁷ And some of them said, "Could not this Man, who opened the eyes of the blind, also have kept this man from dying?"

³⁸ Then Jesus, again groaning in Himself, came to the tomb. It was a cave, and a stone lay against it. ³⁹ Jesus said, "Take away the stone."

Martha, the sister of him who was dead, said to Him, "Lord, by this time there is a stench, for he has been dead four days."

⁴⁰ Jesus said to her, "Did I not say to you that if you would believe you would see the glory of God?" ⁴¹ Then they took away the stone from the place where the dead man was lying. And Jesus lifted up His eyes and said, "Father, I thank You that You have heard Me. ⁴² And I know that You always hear Me, but because of the people who are standing by I said this, that they may believe that You sent Me." ⁴³ Now when He had said these things, He cried with a loud voice, "Lazarus, come forth!" ⁴⁴ And he who had died came out bound hand and foot with graveclothes, and

his face was wrapped with a cloth. Jesus said to them, "Loose him, and let him go."

EXPLORATION

1. How did Mary and Martha react to Jesus' late arrival?

_____

_____

_____

2. How did Mary and Martha differ in the way they expressed their feelings?

_____

_____

_____

3. Do you think Jesus' words to Martha were reassuring to her? Why or why not?

_____

_____

_____

4. How did Martha communicate her belief in Jesus?

_____

_____

_____

5. How did the people react when they saw Jesus weeping over the death of Lazarus?

_____

_____

_____

6. Why do you think Jesus chose to perform this miracle of raising Lazarus from the dead rather than just healing his illness?

_____

_____

_____

INSPIRATION

Martha's words were full of despair. "If you had been here . . ." She stares into the Master's face with confused eyes. She'd been strong long enough; now it hurt too badly. Lazarus was dead. Her brother was gone. And the one man who could have made a difference didn't. He hadn't even made it for the burial. Something about death makes us accuse God of betrayal. "If God were here there would be no death!" we claim . . .

Jesus wasn't angry at Martha. Perhaps it was his patience that caused her to change her tone from frustration to earnestness. "Even now God will give you whatever you ask."

Jesus then made one of those claims that place him either on the throne or in the asylum: "Your brother will rise again."

Martha misunderstood. (Who wouldn't have?) "I know he will rise again in the resurrection at the last day."

That wasn't what Jesus meant. Don't miss the context of the next words. Imagine the setting: Jesus has intruded on the enemy's turf; he's standing in Satan's territory, Death Canyon. His stomach turns as he smells the sulfuric stench of the ex-angel, and he winces as he hears the oppressed wails of those trapped in the prison. Satan has been here. He has violated one of God's creations.

With his foot planted on the serpent's head, Jesus speaks loudly enough that his words echo off the canyon walls. "I am the resurrection and the life. The one who believes in me will live, even though they die; and whoever lives by believing in me will never die" (John 11:25–26). It is the hinge point in history. A chink has been found in death's armor. The keys to the halls of hell have been claimed . . .

With eyes locked on hers, Jesus asks the greatest question found in Scripture, a question meant as much for you and me as for Martha: "Do you believe this?"

Wham! There it is. The bottom line. The dimension that separates Jesus from a thousand gurus and prophets who have come down the pike. The question that drives any responsible listener to absolute obedience or to total rejection of the Christian faith.

"Do you believe this?"

Let the question sink into your heart for a minute. Do you believe that a young, penniless itinerant is larger than your death? Do you truly believe that death is nothing more than an entrance ramp to a new highway? . . .

This is a canyon question. A question which makes sense only during an all-night vigil or in the stillness of smoke-filled waiting rooms. A question that makes sense when all of our props, crutches, and costumes are taken away. For then we must face ourselves as we really are: rudderless humans tail-spinning toward disaster. And we are forced to see Jesus for what he claims to be: our only hope. (From *God Came Near* by Max Lucado.)

REACTION

7. How did Martha's response demonstrate both faith and a lack of faith in Jesus?

_____

_____

_____

_____

8. How was Jesus "intruding on the enemy's turf" in this story?

_____

_____

_____

_____

9. How do Jesus' words and actions in this passage comfort you?

_____

_____

_____

10. How do Jesus' words and actions in this passage challenge you to have greater faith in him?

_____

_____

_____

11. How has God helped you during a recent time of loss or disappointment?

_____

_____

_____

12. How can you share the pain of others in your life who suffer?

_____

_____

_____

LIFE LESSONS

Grief often spawns blame. Tiny fingerlings of fault suggest themselves to us. Someone we love dies. Perhaps we feel it was our fault. Maybe we feel it was someone else's fault. And if no appropriate guilty party accepts the blame, then there's always God. We sometimes are so busy assigning blame that we miss the point of death's inevitability and the genuine hope of resurrection. Jesus used the death of one friend and the sorrow of two others to demonstrate for all time that real life is more than this plane of existence, as sweet and wonderful as this one can be. It was not meant to be the whole meal but a foretaste of things eternal.

DEVOTION

Father, thank you for caring about our pain and disappointments. Calm the whirling winds of fear and hurt that threaten our faith. Keep us from trying to cope with our struggles by our own strength and willpower. Help us to release our emotions to you and trust you to sustain us. Thank you for your comforting words of wisdom. Let us receive the healing of the Holy Spirit.

JOURNALING

How will you surrender your past hurts and disappointments to God?

_____

_____

_____

_____

_____

_____

_____

_____

_____

_____

_____

_____

FOR FURTHER READING

To complete the book of John during this twelve-part study, read John 11:1–12:50. For more Bible passages dealing with hurts, read Matthew 9:36; 11:28–30; Romans 12:15; and 2 Corinthians 1:3–7.

THE MASTER SERVANT

"I have set you an example that you should do as I have done for you. Very truly I tell you, no servant is greater than his master, nor is a messenger greater than the one who sent him."
JOHN 13:15–16

REFLECTION

Someone has wisely observed that being a servant is fine until some-one starts treating you like one. We don't naturally gravitate toward servanthood. Helping others has a certain charm, as long as it doesn't inconvenience or cost too much. But genuine servanthood is about being put upon. Authentic service is sparked by the immediate need, not the convenience of energy, schedule, or especially social norms and expec-tations. Think of a special time when you enjoyed fellowship with other believers. What aspects of service can you identify in that setting? How did the presence of service cause you to enjoy that fellowship so much?

_____

_____

_____

_____

_____

_____

_____

_____

_____

_____

_____

SITUATION

The Gospels record a number of things that Jesus said and did on the night he was betrayed. What they all reveal, however, is that he stayed on message and on task even as his time on earth was coming to an end. He was about to show his disciples how much he loved them by dying for them, but before that, he wanted to demonstrate how much he loved them in a simple, practical, and profound way.

OBSERVATION

Read John 13:1–20 from the New International
Version or the New King James Version.

NEW INTERNATIONAL VERSION

[1] It was just before the Passover Festival. Jesus knew that the hour had come for him to leave this world and go to the Father. Having loved his own who were in the world, he loved them to the end.

[2] The evening meal was in progress, and the devil had already prompted Judas, the son of Simon Iscariot, to betray Jesus. [3] Jesus knew that the Father had put all things under his power, and that he had come from God and was returning to God; [4] so he got up from the meal, took off his outer clothing, and wrapped a towel around his waist. [5] After that, he poured water into a basin and began to wash his disciples' feet, drying them with the towel that was wrapped around him.

[6] He came to Simon Peter, who said to him, "Lord, are you going to wash my feet?"

[7] Jesus replied, "You do not realize now what I am doing, but later you will understand."

[8] "No," said Peter, "you shall never wash my feet."

Jesus answered, "Unless I wash you, you have no part with me."

[9] "Then, Lord," Simon Peter replied, "not just my feet but my hands and my head as well!"

[10] Jesus answered, "Those who have had a bath need only to wash their feet; their whole body is clean. And you are clean, though not every one of you." [11] For he knew who was going to betray him, and that was why he said not every one was clean.

[12] When he had finished washing their feet, he put on his clothes and returned to his place. "Do you understand what I have done for you?" he asked them. [13] "You call me 'Teacher' and 'Lord,' and rightly so, for that is what I am. [14] Now that I, your Lord and Teacher, have washed your feet, you also should wash one another's feet. [15] I have set you an example that

you should do as I have done for you. ¹⁶ Very truly I tell you, no servant is greater than his master, nor is a messenger greater than the one who sent him. ¹⁷ Now that you know these things, you will be blessed if you do them.

¹⁸ "I am not referring to all of you; I know those I have chosen. But this is to fulfill this passage of Scripture: 'He who shared my bread has turned against me.'

¹⁹ "I am telling you now before it happens, so that when it does happen you will believe that I am who I am. ²⁰ Very truly I tell you, whoever accepts anyone I send accepts me; and whoever accepts me accepts the one who sent me."

NEW KING JAMES VERSION

¹ Now before the Feast of the Passover, when Jesus knew that His hour had come that He should depart from this world to the Father, having loved His own who were in the world, He loved them to the end.

² And supper being ended, the devil having already put it into the heart of Judas Iscariot, Simon's son, to betray Him, ³ Jesus, knowing that the Father had given all things into His hands, and that He had come from God and was going to God, ⁴ rose from supper and laid aside His garments, took a towel and girded Himself. ⁵ After that, He poured water into a basin and began to wash the disciples' feet, and to wipe them with the towel with which He was girded. ⁶ Then He came to Simon Peter. And Peter said to Him, "Lord, are You washing my feet?"

⁷ Jesus answered and said to him, "What I am doing you do not understand now, but you will know after this."

⁸ Peter said to Him, "You shall never wash my feet!"

Jesus answered him, "If I do not wash you, you have no part with Me."

⁹ Simon Peter said to Him, "Lord, not my feet only, but also my hands and my head!"

¹⁰ Jesus said to him, "He who is bathed needs only to wash his feet, but is completely clean; and you are clean, but not all of you." ¹¹ For He knew who would betray Him; therefore He said, "You are not all clean."

[12] So when He had washed their feet, taken His garments, and sat down again, He said to them, "Do you know what I have done to you? [13] You call Me Teacher and Lord, and you say well, for so I am. [14] If I then, your Lord and Teacher, have washed your feet, you also ought to wash one another's feet. [15] For I have given you an example, that you should do as I have done to you. [16] Most assuredly, I say to you, a servant is not greater than his master; nor is he who is sent greater than he who sent him. [17] If you know these things, blessed are you if you do them.

[18] "I do not speak concerning all of you. I know whom I have chosen; but that the Scripture may be fulfilled, 'He who eats bread with Me has lifted up his heel against Me.' [19] Now I tell you before it comes, that when it does come to pass, you may believe that I am He. [20] Most assuredly, I say to you, he who receives whomever I send receives Me; and he who receives Me receives Him who sent Me."

EXPLORATION

1. What do you suppose the atmosphere was like at this meal?

_____

_____

_____

2. What range of feelings did Jesus have for his disciples?

_____

_____

_____

_____

3. How did Jesus show his love for his friends?

_____

_____

_____

_____

4. What was Simon Peter's immediate reaction to being served by Jesus?

_____

_____

_____

5. Why was it difficult for Simon Peter to accept Jesus' service?

_____

_____

_____

6. What reason did Jesus give to the disciples for performing this act of service?

_____

_____

_____

INSPIRATION

It has been a long day. Jerusalem is packed with Passover guests, most of whom clamor for a glimpse of the Teacher. The spring sun is warm. The streets are dry. And the disciples are a long way from home. A splash of cool water would be refreshing.

The disciples enter, one by one, and take their places around the table. On the wall hangs a towel, and on the floor sits a pitcher and a basin. Any one of the disciples could volunteer for the job, but not one does.

After a few moments, Jesus stands and removes his outer garment. He wraps a servant's girdle around his waist, takes up the basin, and kneels before one of the disciples. He unlaces a sandal and gently lifts the foot and places it in the basin, covers it with water, and begins to bathe it. One by one; one grimy foot after another, Jesus works his way down the row.

In Jesus' day the washing of feet was a task reserved not just for servants but for the lowest of servants. Every circle has its pecking order, and the circle of household workers was no exception. The servant at the bottom of the totem pole was expected to be the one on his knees with the towel and basin.

In this case the one with the towel and basin is the King of the universe. Hands that shaped the stars now wash away filth. Fingers that formed mountains now massage toes. And the one before whom all nations will one day kneel now kneels before his disciples. Hours before his own death, Jesus' concern is singular. He wants his disciples to know how much he loves them. More than removing dirt, Jesus is removing doubt. (From *Just Like Jesus* by Max Lucado.)

REACTION

7. What long-term impact do you think Jesus' actions had on the disciples?

_____

_____

_____

8. When has the humble service of a fellow believer inspired you?

_____

_____

_____

9. What are some of the rewards of serving others?

_____

_____

_____

10. Why is it important for believers to have fellowship with each other?

_____

_____

_____

11. How does it affect you to see people serving with humility in the church?

_____

_____

_____

_____

_____

12. When have you found it difficult to accept help from a fellow believer? Why?

_____

_____

_____

_____

_____

LIFE LESSONS

What if we serve and no one notices? What if we help and no one seems to care? What if we offer to serve and are rejected? Welcome to the servant's world. Jesus never predicted how the servees would respond; he simply placed his actions before us as an example. We need to pray for alertness to the opportunities God presents to us to serve and the wisdom to respond as Jesus would. At the same time, we need to learn to express gratitude to Jesus for his immeasurable act of service in going to the cross for us.

DEVOTION

Father, in Jesus we see the perfect model of humble service. Help us to be like him. Open our eyes to the needs of others in the world, and give us the strength and motivation to act when we see those needs. Help us to follow your Word. Help us to follow in Christ's footsteps.

JOURNALING

What practical things can you do today to better serve others?

FOR FURTHER READING

To complete the book of John during this twelve-part study, read John 13:1–14:14. For more Bible passages on serving, read Matthew 20:25–28; Ephesians 6:7; Galatians 5:13; and Philippians 2:7.

JESUS' PRAYER

"O righteous Father! The world has not known You, but I have known You; and these have known that You sent Me. And I have declared to them Your name, and will declare it, that the love with which You loved Me may be in them, and I in them."

JOHN 17:25–26 NKJV

REFLECTION

Hearing someone pray for us by name can have a deep and lasting effect. It's humbling and wonderful to know that someone is actually thinking about us and that our name has been mentioned in God's presence. We can return the favor. Whether or not they hear us, we can make it a habit to include thoughtful prayer for others when we bow before God. Think for a moment about how you pray for others. What, if anything, needs to change?

_____

_____

_____

_____

_____

SITUATION

The events in John 13–17 occurred during a meal that Jesus had with his disciples, known as the "Last Supper," on the final evening of Jesus' ministry on earth. In light of his approaching betrayal and death, Jesus prayed for his followers. Although the Gospels contain many references to Jesus praying, this is the longest example of the way Jesus talked with his Father.

OBSERVATION

Read John 17:1–26 from the New International Version or the New King James Version.

NEW INTERNATIONAL VERSION

¹ After Jesus said this, he looked toward heaven and prayed:

"Father, the hour has come. Glorify your Son, that your Son may glorify you. ² For you granted him authority over all people that he might give eternal life to all those you have given him. ³ Now this is eternal life: that they know you, the only true God, and Jesus Christ, whom you have sent. ⁴ I have brought you glory on earth by finishing the work you gave me to do. ⁵ And now, Father, glorify me in your presence with the glory I had with you before the world began.

⁶ "I have revealed you to those whom you gave me out of the world. They were yours; you gave them to me and they have obeyed your word. ⁷ Now they know that everything you have given me comes from you. ⁸ For I gave them the words you gave me and they accepted them. They knew with certainty that I came from you, and they believed that you sent me. ⁹ I pray for them. I am not praying for the world, but for those you have given me, for they are yours. ¹⁰ All I have is yours, and all you have is mine. And glory has come to me through them. ¹¹ I will remain in the world no longer, but they are still in the world, and I am coming to you. Holy Father, protect them by the power of your name, the name you gave me, so that they may be one as we are one. ¹² While I was with them, I protected them and kept them safe by that name you gave me. None has been lost except the one doomed to destruction so that Scripture would be fulfilled.

¹³ "I am coming to you now, but I say these things while I am still in the world, so that they may have the full measure of my joy within them. ¹⁴ I have given them your word and the world has hated them, for they are not of the world any more than I am of the world. ¹⁵ My prayer is not that you take them out of the world but that you protect them from the evil one. ¹⁶ They are not of the world, even as I am not of it. ¹⁷ Sanctify them by the truth; your word is truth. ¹⁸ As you sent me into the world, I have sent them into the world. ¹⁹ For them I sanctify myself, that they too may be truly sanctified.

²⁰ "My prayer is not for them alone. I pray also for those who will believe in me through their message, ²¹ that all of them may be one, Father, just as you are in me and I am in you. May they also be in us so that the world may believe that you have sent me. ²² I have given them the glory that you gave me, that they may be one as we are one— ²³ I in them

and you in me—so that they may be brought to complete unity. Then the world will know that you sent me and have loved them even as you have loved me.

[24] "Father, I want those you have given me to be with me where I am, and to see my glory, the glory you have given me because you loved me before the creation of the world.

[25] "Righteous Father, though the world does not know you, I know you, and they know that you have sent me. [26] I have made you known to them, and will continue to make you known in order that the love you have for me may be in them and that I myself may be in them."

New King James Version

[1] Jesus spoke these words, lifted up His eyes to heaven, and said: "Father, the hour has come. Glorify Your Son, that Your Son also may glorify You, [2] as You have given Him authority over all flesh, that He should give eternal life to as many as You have given Him. [3] And this is eternal life, that they may know You, the only true God, and Jesus Christ whom You have sent. [4] I have glorified You on the earth. I have finished the work which You have given Me to do. [5] And now, O Father, glorify Me together with Yourself, with the glory which I had with You before the world was.

[6] "I have manifested Your name to the men whom You have given Me out of the world. They were Yours, You gave them to Me, and they have kept Your word. [7] Now they have known that all things which You have given Me are from You. [8] For I have given to them the words which You have given Me; and they have received them, and have known surely that I came forth from You; and they have believed that You sent Me.

[9] "I pray for them. I do not pray for the world but for those whom You have given Me, for they are Yours. [10] And all Mine are Yours, and Yours are Mine, and I am glorified in them. [11] Now I am no longer in the world, but these are in the world, and I come to You. Holy Father, keep through Your name those whom You have given Me, that they may be one as We are. [12] While I was with them in the world, I kept them in Your name.

Those whom You gave Me I have kept; and none of them is lost except the son of perdition, that the Scripture might be fulfilled. [13] But now I come to You, and these things I speak in the world, that they may have My joy fulfilled in themselves. [14] I have given them Your word; and the world has hated them because they are not of the world, just as I am not of the world. [15] I do not pray that You should take them out of the world, but that You should keep them from the evil one. [16] They are not of the world, just as I am not of the world. [17] Sanctify them by Your truth. Your word is truth. [18] As You sent Me into the world, I also have sent them into the world. [19] And for their sakes I sanctify Myself, that they also may be sanctified by the truth.

[20] "I do not pray for these alone, but also for those who will believe in Me through their word; [21] that they all may be one, as You, Father, are in Me, and I in You; that they also may be one in Us, that the world may believe that You sent Me. [22] And the glory which You gave Me I have given them, that they may be one just as We are one: [23] I in them, and You in Me; that they may be made perfect in one, and that the world may know that You have sent Me, and have loved them as You have loved Me.

[24] "Father, I desire that they also whom You gave Me may be with Me where I am, that they may behold My glory which You have given Me; for You loved Me before the foundation of the world. [25] O righteous Father! The world has not known You, but I have known You; and these have known that You sent Me. [26] And I have declared to them Your name, and will declare it, that the love with which You loved Me may be in them, and I in them."

EXPLORATION

1. What was Jesus' request to the Father at the beginning of his prayer (see verses 1–5)?

_____

_____

_____

2. What did Jesus ask the Father to do for his disciples (see verses 6–19)?

_____

_____

_____

3. What did Jesus ask the Father to do for all believers in him (see verses 20–26)?

_____

_____

_____

4. How does this prayer depict Jesus' relationship with God the Father?

_____

_____

_____

5. What spiritual battle does Jesus describe in his prayer?

_____

_____

_____

6. How are believers equipped for this battle?

_____

_____

_____

INSPIRATION

Why do Jesus and his angels rejoice over one repenting sinner? Can they see something we can't? Do they know something we don't? Absolutely. They know what heaven holds. They've seen the table, and they've heard the music, and they can't wait to see your face when you arrive. Better still, they can't wait to see you.

When you arrive and enter the party, something wonderful will happen. A final transformation will occur. You will be just like Jesus. Drink deeply from 1 John 3:2: "What we will be has not yet been made known. But we know that when Christ appears, *we* shall be like him" (emphasis mine).

Of all the blessings of heaven, one of the greatest will be you! You will be God's magnum opus, his work of art. The angels will gasp. God's work will be completed. At last, you will have a heart like his.

You will love with a perfect love. You will worship with a radiant face. You'll hear each word God speaks.

Your heart will be pure, your words will be like jewels, your thoughts will be like treasures.

You will be just like Jesus. You will, at long last, have a heart like his. Envision the heart of Jesus and you'll be envisioning your own. Guiltless. Fearless. Thrilled and joyous. Tirelessly worshipping. Flawlessly discerning. As the mountain stream is pristine and endless, so will be your heart. *You will be like him.*

And if that were not enough, everyone else will be like him as well . . .

Heaven is populated by those who let God change them. Arguments will cease, for jealousy won't exist. Suspicions won't surface, for there will be no secrets. Every sin is gone. Every insecurity is forgotten. Every fear is past. Pure wheat. No weeds. Pure gold. No alloy. Pure love. No lust. Pure hope. No fear. No wonder the angels rejoice when one sinner repents; they know another work of art will soon grace the gallery of God. They know what heaven holds. (From *Just Like Jesus* by Max Lucado.)

REACTION

7. What are some of the daily pressures you face? Rank them from 1 to 10, with 1 being lightest and 10 being the heaviest.

_____

_____

_____

8. How does Jesus' prayer encourage you to face those pressures?

_____

_____

_____

9. What tends to interfere with your prayer life? How have you sought to overcome this?

_____

_____

_____

10. How do you overcome feelings of discouragement when your prayers seem to go unanswered?

_____

_____

_____

11. What can you learn from this passage about the purpose and practice of prayer?

_____

_____

_____

12. How has prayer affected your life and the lives of the people around you?

_____

_____

_____

LIFE LESSONS

If you are a follower of Jesus, you are an answer to his long-ago prayer. You are one of those who have believed because of the faithfulness of others. There is an unbroken chain of witnesses from that upper room to your heart and mind, just as he expected. The faith is in your hands and in your life. Ironically, you keep it by giving it away. If you hold it privately and secretly, you haven't kept it. So pray for the people in your life, and then tell them about Jesus.

DEVOTION

Father, your Son showed us how to pray. He prayed in the morning, he prayed in the evening, he prayed alone, and he prayed with others. In hours of distress he retreated into times of prayer. In hours of joy he lifted his heart to you. Help us to pray in this same way and to make prayer a priority in our daily lives.

JOURNALING

How can you be more involved in the ministry of prayer?

FOR FURTHER READING

To complete the book of John during this twelve-part study, read John 14:15–17:26. For more Bible passages on prayer, read Deuteronomy 4:7; Psalm 32:6; Matthew 14:23; 26:36; Luke 6:28; and Ephesians 6:18.

THE RISEN CHRIST

*"Do not hold on to me, for I have not yet ascended
to the Father. Go instead to my brothers and
tell them, 'I am ascending to my Father and
your Father, to my God and your God.'"*

JOHN 20:17

REFLECTION

If you only listen to the media news reports, the expression "good news" sounds like an oxymoron. It seems that much of what is called "news" is only the bad, tragic, or shocking stories. This makes it all the more crucial to realize that those of us who know the ultimate "good news" have a wonderful opportunity to bring hope to lost and desperate people. What is the best news you have heard recently? Why was this good news for you?

_____

_____

_____

_____

SITUATION

Each of the Gospel accounts makes it clear that Jesus' followers were not expecting anything to happen the morning of the Resurrection. It started out as just another day of grief and confusion after Jesus' arrest, trial, conviction, and crucifixion. Jesus had been placed in a tomb, and the conclusion of the Sabbath made it possible for some of the women to visit in hopes of doing a better job of wrapping and anointing the body. We don't know how Mary and her companions planned to open the tomb, but they certainly didn't anticipate what they found.

OBSERVATION

Read John 20:1–18 from the New International
Version or the New King James Version.

NEW INTERNATIONAL VERSION
¹ Early on the first day of the week, while it was still dark, Mary Magdalene went to the tomb and saw that the stone had been removed

from the entrance.[2] So she came running to Simon Peter and the other disciple, the one Jesus loved, and said, "They have taken the Lord out of the tomb, and we don't know where they have put him!"

[3] So Peter and the other disciple started for the tomb. [4] Both were running, but the other disciple outran Peter and reached the tomb first. [5] He bent over and looked in at the strips of linen lying there but did not go in. [6] Then Simon Peter came along behind him and went straight into the tomb. He saw the strips of linen lying there, [7] as well as the cloth that had been wrapped around Jesus' head. The cloth was still lying in its place, separate from the linen. [8] Finally the other disciple, who had reached the tomb first, also went inside. He saw and believed. [9] (They still did not understand from Scripture that Jesus had to rise from the dead.) [10] Then the disciples went back to where they were staying.

[11] Now Mary stood outside the tomb crying. As she wept, she bent over to look into the tomb [12] and saw two angels in white, seated where Jesus' body had been, one at the head and the other at the foot.

[13] They asked her, "Woman, why are you crying?"

"They have taken my Lord away," she said, "and I don't know where they have put him." [14] At this, she turned around and saw Jesus standing there, but she did not realize that it was Jesus.

[15] He asked her, "Woman, why are you crying? Who is it you are looking for?"

Thinking he was the gardener, she said, "Sir, if you have carried him away, tell me where you have put him, and I will get him."

[16] Jesus said to her, "Mary."

She turned toward him and cried out in Aramaic, "Rabboni!" (which means "Teacher").

[17] Jesus said, "Do not hold on to me, for I have not yet ascended to the Father. Go instead to my brothers and tell them, 'I am ascending to my Father and your Father, to my God and your God.'"

[18] Mary Magdalene went to the disciples with the news: "I have seen the Lord!" And she told them that he had said these things to her.

[1] Now on the first day of the week Mary Magdalene went to the tomb early, while it was still dark, and saw that the stone had been taken away from the tomb. [2] Then she ran and came to Simon Peter, and to the other disciple, whom Jesus loved, and said to them, "They have taken away the Lord out of the tomb, and we do not know where they have laid Him."

[3] Peter therefore went out, and the other disciple, and were going to the tomb. [4] So they both ran together, and the other disciple outran Peter and came to the tomb first. [5] And he, stooping down and looking in, saw the linen cloths lying there; yet he did not go in. [6] Then Simon Peter came, following him, and went into the tomb; and he saw the linen cloths lying there, [7] and the handkerchief that had been around His head, not lying with the linen cloths, but folded together in a place by itself. [8] Then the other disciple, who came to the tomb first, went in also; and he saw and believed. [9] For as yet they did not know the Scripture, that He must rise again from the dead. [10] Then the disciples went away again to their own homes.

[11] But Mary stood outside by the tomb weeping, and as she wept she stooped down and looked into the tomb. [12] And she saw two angels in white sitting, one at the head and the other at the feet, where the body of Jesus had lain. [13] Then they said to her, "Woman, why are you weeping?"

She said to them, "Because they have taken away my Lord, and I do not know where they have laid Him."

[14] Now when she had said this, she turned around and saw Jesus standing there, and did not know that it was Jesus. [15] Jesus said to her, "Woman, why are you weeping? Whom are you seeking?"

She, supposing Him to be the gardener, said to Him, "Sir, if You have carried Him away, tell me where You have laid Him, and I will take Him away."

[16] Jesus said to her, "Mary!"

She turned and said to Him, "Rabboni!" (which is to say, Teacher).

[17] Jesus said to her, "Do not cling to Me, for I have not yet ascended to My Father; but go to My brethren and say to them, 'I am ascending to My Father and your Father, and to My God and your God.'"

¹⁸ Mary Magdalene came and told the disciples that she had seen the Lord, and that He had spoken these things to her.

EXPLORATION

1. At what time of day did Mary visit Jesus' tomb? Why do you think she chose that time?

_____

_____

_____

2. How did Mary react when she saw the stone had been moved from the tomb?

_____

_____

_____

3. How did Mary share the good news she received?

_____

_____

_____

4. How did Peter and the other disciple react when they heard the stone had been removed?

_____

_____

_____

5. What was Mary's concern when she saw the two angels in white in the tomb?

_____

_____

_____

6. How did Jesus reveal himself to Mary? What were his instructions to her?

_____

_____

_____

INSPIRATION

The empty tomb never resists honest investigation. A lobotomy is not a prerequisite of discipleship. Following Christ demands faith, but not blind faith. "Come and see," the angel invites. Shall we?

Take a look at the vacated tomb. Did you know the opponents of Christ never challenged its vacancy? No Pharisee or Roman soldier ever led a contingent back to the burial site and declared, "The angel was wrong. The body is here. It was all a rumor."

They would have if they could have. Within weeks disciples occupied every Jerusalem street corner, announcing a risen Christ. What quicker way for the enemies of the church to shut them up than to produce a cold and lifeless body? Display the cadaver, and Christianity is stillborn. But they had no cadaver to display.

This helps explain the Jerusalem revival. When the apostles argued for the empty tomb, the people looked to the Pharisees for a rebuttal. But they had none to give. As A.M. Fairbairn put it long ago, "The silence of the Jews is as eloquent as the speech of the Christians!"

Speaking of the Christians, remember the followers' fear at the crucifixion? They ran. Scared as cats in a dog pound. Peter cursed Christ at the fire. Emmaus-bound disciples bemoaned the death of Christ on the trail. After the crucifixion, "the disciples were meeting behind locked doors because they were afraid of the Jewish leaders" (John 20:19 NLT).

These guys were so chicken we could call the Upper Room a henhouse.

But fast-forward forty days. Bankrupt traitors have become a force of life-changing fury. Peter is preaching in the very precinct where Christ was arrested. Followers of Christ defy the enemies of Christ. Whip them and they'll worship. Lock them up and they'll launch a jailhouse ministry. As bold after the Resurrection as they were cowardly before it.

Explanation:

Greed? They made no money.

Power? They gave all the credit to Christ.

Popularity? Most were killed for their beliefs.

Only one explanation remains—*a resurrected Christ and his Holy Spirit.* The courage of these men and women was forged in the fire of the empty tomb. The disciples did not dream up a resurrection. The Resurrection fired up the disciples. Have doubts about the empty tomb? Come and see the disciples. (From *Next Door Savior* by Max Lucado.)

REACTION

7. Why is Christ's resurrection important for believers? How would Christianity look without the resurrection?

_____

_____

_____

_____

8. Why do you think it is so hard for some people to believe that Jesus rose from the dead?

_____

_____

_____

9. What does Christ's resurrection mean to you?

_____

_____

_____

10. What evidence helps you believe that Jesus rose from the dead?

_____

_____

_____

11. What tends to prevent you from sharing the exciting news of Christ's resurrection with those who don't believe?

_____

_____

_____

12. What objections do people raise about Christ's resurrection? How can you respond?

_____

_____

_____

LIFE LESSONS

The personal importance and impact of Jesus' resurrection is illustrated by the disciples' lives and spelled out in passages such as 1 Corinthians 15. The basis of forgiveness takes us back to Christ's death, but the guarantee of all the promises and the hope we live by depends on the truth of the empty tomb. Authentic believers are forever overwhelmed by two conclusions: _Jesus died for me_ and _Jesus rose again for me._ In those two statements rests a hope large enough for life and stronger than death.

DEVOTION

Jesus, we thank you for the sweet surprise of Easter morning. We thank you that when you rose from the dead, you didn't go immediately to heaven but visited people. This visit of love reminds us that people were the reason you died. We praise your name for that sweet surprise.

JOURNALING

How does the victory of Christ's resurrection bring victory to your life?

FOR FURTHER READING

To complete the book of John during this twelve-part study, read John 18:1–20:18. For more Bible passages on the Resurrection, read Matthew 22:31–32; Acts 1:22; 4:2, 33; Romans 1:4; 6:5; and 1 Peter 1:3.

PETER'S SECOND CHANCE

He said to him the third time, "Simon, son of Jonah, do you love Me?" Peter was grieved because He said to him the third time, "Do you love Me?" And he said to Him, "Lord, You know all things; You know that I love You." Jesus said to him, "Feed My sheep."

JOHN 21:17 NKJV

REFLECTION

Betrayal, disagreement, misunderstanding, and even exhaustion can fracture a relationship. Firsthand experience in these painful situations often makes us feel that broken relationships are beyond repair. But God reminds us that what we conclude is impossible, he makes possible every day. Think of a time when you helped restore a broken relationship. How were you able to help in that situation?

_____

_____

_____

_____

SITUATION

For at least one person, the joy of Jesus' resurrection was overshadowed by shame. Peter remembered his failure. After boldly proclaiming that he would never forsake Jesus, he had to eat his words just hours later when—not once, but *three times*—he denied knowing Jesus. Jesus' resurrection suddenly gave him a new perspective. The question that must have lingered in Peter's mind was whether or not Jesus would give him a second chance. Eventually, Jesus drew Peter aside for a heart-to-heart talk over breakfast.

OBSERVATION

Read John 21:1–19 from the New International Version or the New King James Version.

New International Version
¹ Afterward Jesus appeared again to his disciples, by the Sea of Galilee. It happened this way: ² Simon Peter, Thomas (also known as Didymus),

Nathanael from Cana in Galilee, the sons of Zebedee, and two other disciples were together.³ "I'm going out to fish," Simon Peter told them, and they said, "We'll go with you." So they went out and got into the boat, but that night they caught nothing.

⁴ Early in the morning, Jesus stood on the shore, but the disciples did not realize that it was Jesus.

⁵ He called out to them, "Friends, haven't you any fish?"

"No," they answered.

⁶ He said, "Throw your net on the right side of the boat and you will find some." When they did, they were unable to haul the net in because of the large number of fish.

⁷ Then the disciple whom Jesus loved said to Peter, "It is the Lord!" As soon as Simon Peter heard him say, "It is the Lord," he wrapped his outer garment around him (for he had taken it off) and jumped into the water. ⁸ The other disciples followed in the boat, towing the net full of fish, for they were not far from shore, about a hundred yards. ⁹ When they landed, they saw a fire of burning coals there with fish on it, and some bread.

¹⁰ Jesus said to them, "Bring some of the fish you have just caught." ¹¹ So Simon Peter climbed back into the boat and dragged the net ashore. It was full of large fish, 153, but even with so many the net was not torn. ¹² Jesus said to them, "Come and have breakfast." None of the disciples dared ask him, "Who are you?" They knew it was the Lord. ¹³ Jesus came, took the bread and gave it to them, and did the same with the fish. ¹⁴ This was now the third time Jesus appeared to his disciples after he was raised from the dead.

¹⁵ When they had finished eating, Jesus said to Simon Peter, "Simon son of John, do you love me more than these?"

"Yes, Lord," he said, "you know that I love you."

Jesus said, "Feed my lambs."

¹⁶ Again Jesus said, "Simon son of John, do you love me?"

He answered, "Yes, Lord, you know that I love you."

Jesus said, "Take care of my sheep."

¹⁷ The third time he said to him, "Simon son of John, do you love me?"

Peter was hurt because Jesus asked him the third time, "Do you love me?" He said, "Lord, you know all things; you know that I love you."

Jesus said, "Feed my sheep. [18] Very truly I tell you, when you were younger you dressed yourself and went where you wanted; but when you are old you will stretch out your hands, and someone else will dress you and lead you where you do not want to go." [19] Jesus said this to indicate the kind of death by which Peter would glorify God. Then he said to him, "Follow me!"

NEW KING JAMES VERSION

[1] After these things Jesus showed Himself again to the disciples at the Sea of Tiberias, and in this way He showed Himself: [2] Simon Peter, Thomas called the Twin, Nathanael of Cana in Galilee, the sons of Zebedee, and two others of His disciples were together. [3] Simon Peter said to them, "I am going fishing."

They said to him, "We are going with you also." They went out and immediately got into the boat, and that night they caught nothing. [4] But when the morning had now come, Jesus stood on the shore; yet the disciples did not know that it was Jesus. [5] Then Jesus said to them, "Children, have you any food?"

They answered Him, "No."

[6] And He said to them, "Cast the net on the right side of the boat, and you will find some." So they cast, and now they were not able to draw it in because of the multitude of fish.

[7] Therefore that disciple whom Jesus loved said to Peter, "It is the Lord!" Now when Simon Peter heard that it was the Lord, he put on his outer garment (for he had removed it), and plunged into the sea. [8] But the other disciples came in the little boat (for they were not far from land, but about two hundred cubits), dragging the net with fish. [9] Then, as soon as they had come to land, they saw a fire of coals there, and fish laid on it, and bread. [10] Jesus said to them, "Bring some of the fish which you have just caught."

[11] Simon Peter went up and dragged the net to land, full of large fish, one hundred and fifty-three; and although there were so many, the net was not broken. [12] Jesus said to them, "Come and eat breakfast." Yet none

of the disciples dared ask Him, "Who are You?"—knowing that it was the Lord. [13] Jesus then came and took the bread and gave it to them, and likewise the fish.

[14] This is now the third time Jesus showed Himself to His disciples after He was raised from the dead.

[15] So when they had eaten breakfast, Jesus said to Simon Peter, "Simon, son of Jonah, do you love Me more than these?"

He said to Him, "Yes, Lord; You know that I love You."

He said to him, "Feed My lambs."

[16] He said to him again a second time, "Simon, son of Jonah, do you love Me?"

He said to Him, "Yes, Lord; You know that I love You."

He said to him, "Tend My sheep."

[17] He said to him the third time, "Simon, son of Jonah, do you love Me?" Peter was grieved because He said to him the third time, "Do you love Me?"

And he said to Him, "Lord, You know all things; You know that I love You."

Jesus said to him, "Feed My sheep. [18] Most assuredly, I say to you, when you were younger, you girded yourself and walked where you wished; but when you are old, you will stretch out your hands, and another will gird you and carry you where you do not wish." [19] This He spoke, signifying by what death he would glorify God. And when He had spoken this, He said to him, "Follow Me."

EXPLORATION

1. Why did Jesus choose to reveal himself to the disciples in this way? (Compare this account with an earlier encounter between Jesus and the disciples in Luke 5:1–11.)

_____

_____

_____

2. In what way did the disciples react when they realized it was Jesus standing on the shore?

_____

_____

_____

_____

3. How did Jesus choose to restore his relationship with Peter?

_____

_____

_____

4. How did Peter respond to Jesus' words and actions?

_____

_____

_____

5. Why do you think Jesus asked Peter three times whether he loved him?

_____

_____

_____

6. How did Jesus emphasize the connection between love and service?

_____

_____

_____

INSPIRATION

The sun was in the water before Peter noticed it—a wavy circle of gold on the surface of the sea. A fisherman is usually the first to spot the sun rising over the crest of the hills. It means his night of labor is finally over.

But not for this fisherman. Though the light reflected on the lake, the darkness lingered in Peter's heart. The wind chilled, but he didn't feel it. His friends slept soundly, but he didn't care . . .

His thoughts were far from the Sea of Galilee. His mind was in Jerusalem, reliving an anguished night. As the boat rocked, his memories raced: the clanking of the Roman guard, the flash of a sword and the duck of a head, a touch for Malchus, a rebuke for Peter, soldiers leading Jesus away.

"What was I thinking?" Peter mumbled to himself as he stared at the bottom of the boat. *Why did I run?*

Peter had run; he had turned his back on his dearest friend and run. We don't know where. Peter may not have known where. He found a hole, a hut, an abandoned shed—he found a place to hide and he hid . . .

So Peter is in the boat, on the lake. Once again he's fished all night. Once again the sea has surrendered nothing.

His thoughts are interrupted by a shout from the shore. "Catch any fish?" Peter and John look up. Probably a villager. "No!" they yell. "Try the other side!" the voice yells back. John looks at Peter. What harm? So out sails the net. Peter wraps the rope around his wrist to wait.

But there is no wait. The rope pulls taut and the net catches. Peter sets his weight against the side of the boat and begins to bring in the net; reaching down, pulling up, reaching down, pulling up. He's so intense with the task, he misses the message.

John doesn't. The moment is *deja vu*. This has happened before. The long night. The empty net. The call to cast again. Fish flapping on the floor of the boat. Wait a minute. He lifts his eyes to the man on the shore. "It's him," he whispers.

Then louder, "It's Jesus."

Then shouting, "It's the Lord, Peter. It's the Lord!"

Peter turns and looks. Jesus has come. Not Jesus the teacher, but Jesus the death-defeater, Jesus King . . . Jesus the victor over darkness. Jesus the God of heaven and earth is on the shore . . .

Peter plunges into the water, swims to the shore, and stumbles out wet and shivering and stands in front of the friend he betrayed. Jesus has prepared a bed of coals. Both are aware of the last time Peter had stood near a fire. Peter had failed God, but God had come to him.

For one of the few times in his life, Peter is silent. What words would suffice? The moment is too holy for words. God is offering breakfast to the friend who betrayed him. And Peter is once again finding grace at Calvary.

What do you say at a moment like this? What do *you* say at a moment such as this?

It's just you and God. You and God both know what you did. And neither of you is proud of it. What do you do?

You might consider doing what Peter did. Stand in God's presence. Stand in his sight. Stand still and wait. Sometimes that's all a soul can do. Too repentant to speak, but too hopeful to leave—we just stand.

Stand amazed. He has come back. He invites you to try again. This time, with him. (From *He Still Moves Stones* by Max Lucado.)

REACTION

7. How can failure destroy a person? How can Jesus restore a person after a fall?

_____

_____

_____

_____

_____

8. What tends to hinder you from accepting and enjoying God's forgiveness?

_____

_____

_____

_____

_____

9. What hope does this story offer to you?

_____

_____

_____

_____

10. How does this story inspire you to handle your mistakes and failures?

_____

_____

_____

_____

11. When have you experienced God's forgiveness in a meaningful way?

_____

_____

_____

_____

12. In what failed relationship would you like to experience healing?

_____

_____

_____

_____

LIFE LESSONS

As you think back over the last few weeks, can you see ways in which God has been bringing about change in your life as you've walked with Jesus? Reflect on the awesome Savior that you follow. Reflect on the personal life lessons you have learned. The Gospel of John closes with hope for Peter and hope for you. There is a future now and forever. God can help you with your failures. Jesus offers you the same quiet, persistent invitation he gave Peter: "Follow me."

DEVOTION

Father, help us as we cope and grapple with yesterday's failures. They weigh us down. Help us to release our regrets to you, Father. And help us to forgive ourselves—even as you have forgiven us—that we might not live burdened and shackled by yesterday's failures. We want to live free by your grace. Help us to follow you, Jesus.

JOURNALING

How can you have the depth of compassion for others that Christ has for you?

_____

_____

_____

_____

_____

_____

_____

_____

_____

_____

_____

FOR FURTHER READING

To complete the book of John during this twelve-part study, read John 20:19–21:25. For more Bible passages on forgiveness, read Psalm 130:3–4; Daniel 9:9; Matthew 6:14–15; Acts 10:43; Ephesians 1:7; Colossians 3:13; and 1 John 1:9.

LEADER'S GUIDE FOR SMALL GROUPS

Thank you for your willingness to lead a group through *Life Lessons from John*. The rewards of being a leader are different from those of participating, and we hope you find your own walk with Jesus deepened by this experience. During the twelve lessons in this study, you will guide your group through selected passages in John and explore the key themes of the Gospel. There are several elements in this leader's guide that will help you as you structure your study and reflection time, so be sure to follow along and take advantage of each one.

BEFORE YOU BEGIN

Before your first meeting, make sure the group members have their own copy of the *Life Lessons from John* study guide so they can follow along and have their answers written out ahead of time. Alternately, you can hand out the guides at your first meeting and give the group some time to look over the material and ask any preliminary questions. Be sure to send a sheet around the room during that first meeting and have the members write down their name, phone number, and email address so you can keep in touch with them during the week.

There are several ways to structure the duration of the study. You can choose to cover each lesson individually for a total of twelve weeks of discussion, or you can combine two lessons together per week for a total of six weeks of discussion. You can also choose to have the group members read just the selected passages of Scripture given in each lesson, or they can cover the entire book of John by reading the material listed in the "For Further Reading" section at the end of each lesson. The following table illustrates these options:

Twelve-Week Format

Week	Lessons Covered	Simplified Reading	Expanded Reading
1	When God Became Man	John 1:1–18	John 1:1–34
2	A Wedding in Cana	John 2:1–11	John 1:35–2:25
3	The Woman at the Well	John 4:5–30	John 3:1–4:42
4	Healing the Sick	John 5:1–15	John 4:43–5:47
5	A Hungry Crowd	John 6:1–15	John 6:1–71
6	A Guilty Woman	John 8:1–11	John 7:1–8:59
7	A Man Born Blind	John 9:1–12	John 9:1–10:42
8	The Loss of a Friend	John 11:17–44	John 11:1–12:50
9	The Master Servant	John 13:1–20	John 13:1–14:14
10	Jesus' Prayer	John 17:1–26	John 14:15–17:26
11	The Risen Christ	John 20:1–18	John 18:1–20:18
12	Peter's Second Chance	John 21:1–19	John 20:19–21:25

Six-Week Format

Week	Lessons Covered	Simplified Reading	Expanded Reading
1	When God Became Man /A Wedding in Cana	John 1:1–18; 2:1–11	John 1:1–2:25
2	The Woman at the Well /Healing the Sick	John 4:5–30; 5:1–15	John 3:1–5:47
3	A Hungry Crowd /A Guilty Woman	John 6:1–15; 8:1–11	John 6:1–8:59
4	A Man Born Blind /The Loss of a Friend	John 9:1–12; 11:17–44	John 9:1–12:50
5	The Master Servant / Jesus' Prayer	John 13:1–20; 17:1–26	John 13:1–17:26
6	The Risen Christ / Peter's Second Chance	John 20:1–18; 21:1–19	John 18:1–21:25

Generally, the ideal size you will want for the group is between eight to ten people, which ensures everyone will have enough time to participate in discussions. If you have more people, you might want to break up the main group into smaller subgroups. Encourage those who show up at the first meeting to commit to attending the duration of the study, as this will help the group members get to know each other, create stability for the group, and help you know how to prepare each week.

Each of the lessons begins with a brief reflection that highlights the theme you will be discussing that week. As you begin your group time, have the group members briefly respond to the opening question to get them thinking about the topic at hand. Some people may want to tell a long story in response to one of these questions, but the goal is to keep the answers brief. Ideally, you want everyone in the group to get a chance to answer, so try to keep the responses to just a few minutes. If you have more talkative group members, say up front that everyone needs to limit his or her answer to two minutes.

Give the group members a chance to answer, but tell them to feel free to pass if they wish. With the rest of the study, it's generally not a good idea to have everyone answer every question—a free-flowing discussion is more desirable. But with the opening reflection question, you can go around the circle. Encourage shy people to share, but don't force them.

Before your first meeting, let the group members know how the lessons are broken down. During your group discussion time the members will be drawing on the answers they wrote to the Exploration and Reaction sections, so encourage them to always complete these ahead of time. Also, invite them to bring any questions and insights they uncovered while reading to your next meeting, especially if they had a breakthrough moment or if they didn't understand something they read.

WEEKLY PREPARATION

As the leader, there are a few things you should do to prepare for each meeting:

- *Read through the lesson.* This will help you to become familiar with the content and know how to structure the discussion times.
- *Decide which questions you want to discuss.* Depending on how you structure your group time, you may not be able to cover every question. So select the questions ahead of time that you absolutely want the group to explore.
- *Be familiar with the questions you want to discuss.* When the group meets you'll be watching the clock, so you want to make sure you are familiar with the Bible study questions you have selected. You can then spend time in the passage again when the group meets. In this way, you'll ensure you have the passage more deeply in your mind than your group members.
- *Pray for your group.* Pray for your group members throughout the week and ask God to lead them as they study his Word.
- *Bring extra supplies to your meeting.* The members should bring their own pens for writing notes, but it's a good idea to have extras available for those who forget. You may also want to bring paper and additional Bibles.

Note that in many cases there will not be one "right" answer to the question. Answers will vary, especially when the group members are being asked to share their personal experiences.

STRUCTURING THE DISCUSSION TIME

You will need to determine with your group how long you want to meet each week so you can plan your time accordingly. Generally, most groups like to meet for either sixty minutes or ninety minutes, so you could use one of the following schedules:

Section	60 Minutes	90 Minutes
WELCOME (members arrive and get settled)	5 minutes	10 minutes
REFLECTION (discuss the opening question for the lesson)	10 minutes	15 minutes
DISCUSSION (discuss the Bible study questions in the Exploration and Reaction sections)	35 minutes	50 minutes
PRAYER/CLOSING (pray together as a group and dismiss)	10 minutes	15 minutes

As the group leader, it is up to you to keep track of the time and keep things moving along according to your schedule. You might want to set a timer for each segment so both you and the group members know when your time is up. (Note that there are some good phone apps for timers that play a gentle chime or other pleasant sound instead of a disruptive noise.) Don't feel pressured to cover every question you have selected if the group has a good discussion going. Again, it's not necessary to go around the circle and make everyone share.

Don't be concerned if the group members are silent or slow to share. People are often quiet when they are pulling together their ideas, and this might be a new experience for them. Just ask a question and let it hang in the air until someone shares. You can then say, "Thank you. What about others? What came to you when you reflected on the passage?"

GROUP DYNAMICS

Leading a group through *Life Lessons from John* will prove to be highly rewarding both to you and your group members—but that doesn't mean you will not encounter any challenges along the way! Discussions can get off track. Group members may not be sensitive to the needs and ideas of others. Some might worry they will be expected to talk about matters that make them feel awkward. Others may express comments that result in disagreements. To help ease this strain on you and the group, consider the following ground rules:

- When someone raises a question or comment that is off the main topic, suggest you deal with it another time, or, if you feel led to go in that direction, let the group know you will be spending some time discussing it.
- If someone asks a question you don't know how to answer, admit it and move on. At your discretion, feel free to invite group members to comment on questions that call for personal experience.
- If you find one or two people are dominating the discussion time, direct a few questions to others in the group. Outside the main group time, ask the more dominating members to help you draw out the quieter ones. Work to make them a part of the solution instead of the problem.
- When a disagreement occurs, encourage the group members to process the matter in love. Encourage those on opposite sides to restate what they heard the other side say about the matter, and then invite each side to evaluate if that perception is accurate. Lead the group in examining other Scriptures related to the topic and look for common ground.

When any of these issues arise, encourage your group members to follow the words from the Bible: "Love one another" (John 13:34), "If it is possible, as far as it depends on you, live at peace with everyone" (Romans 12:18), and, "Be quick to listen, slow to speak and slow to become angry" (James 1:19).

Thank you again for taking the time to lead your group. May God reward your efforts and dedication and make your time together in this study fruitful for his kingdom.